Rogue Scientist

Rogue Scientist

(A Memoir)

*The Creation and Adventures of an
Exploration Geologist*

Jan Cannon, Ph.D.

To order additional copies of this book, contact:
Xlibris
1-888-795-4274
www.Xlibris.com
Orders@Xlibris.com
746975

CONTENTS

The Moon Program 16

A Short Hike in the Grand Canyon 21

Grantsmanship...35

North to Alaska 38

Malaspina Glacier 41

Pictographs...44

Aniakchak Caldera...46

A Floatplane Trip to Sithylemenkat Lake.........................49

The Departure Stall 52

Fort Yukon to Tanana 55

A Loose Cannon in the Arctic...................................59

Snow-Blind 62

The Multiengine Rating..65

The Taxi from Hell 69

A Visit to Anak Krakatoa 72

A Small Nick in the Prop 80

Negative, Three in the Green 87

Down Under and Hot..91

Light Rain, Summer 2013.......................................98

Inertial Drive 101

The Arctic Winter...102

THE BUSH PILOT AT THE BAR 105

I took a swallow of my energy drink, set the can on the table, and stood up so I could reach the master switch on the back of my computer. As I touched the switch with the forefinger on my right hand, a strange feeling occurred in the center of my left hand. An area about the size of a quarter started tingling as if it was going to sleep. I shook my hand, and the tingling sensation began to spiral out across the rest of the hand. I had about two seconds to ponder what was going on when my left foot began to experience similar phenomena. I felt a little dizzy, and my left leg felt wobbly. At this point, my conscious brain made a connection with these symptoms: I was having a stroke!

Thus began the end of my life.

I staggered and fell into the chair and then grabbed the phone and dialed 911. While talking to a female voice, I slid out of the chair and onto the floor, still holding the phone. I told her who I was, where I was, and that I was having a stroke. She assured me that help was on the way. I hung up and called Anita, and by this time, I was having trouble seeing the numbers on the phone. I told Anita what was happening, and she headed to the studio to help. Now everything was black; I was paralyzed and couldn't move. I heard sirens coming toward me. Soon I heard the medics talking to me, and pain was spreading across my body. The pain in my head escalated to unbelievable levels, and I don't remember much more until the next week.

I had a hemorrhagic stroke, which affected the upper right hemisphere and the basal ganglia. The neurologist insisted that it was initiated by the energy drink. Later, I researched this and discovered that such energy drinks were banned in Denmark and Sweden because it was well known that such drinks caused strokes. There was no warning on the can or public notice about such risks. Once again, the corrupt US government had adversely affected me.

It took a year for the pain in the left side of my body and my left arm and leg to go away, but the paralysis lingered on. It interrupted my consulting work in Alaska and ended my quest for a commercial pilot's license for helicopters. Definitely, this was the end of my world.

I missed the thrill of visiting a lonely geologic-sampling site in the remote mountains of Alaska. I missed the challenge of slowly maneuvering a helicopter through a narrow rock canyon and landing on a small gravel bar. Such feelings and challenges were that of which my life has been made.

It is 2016. I have died, but at least the pain is gone. My brain is so full of memories that they seem to be leaking out from the edges.

Some of my earliest memories were of wanting to fly. I finally got there, but it was a long and arduous road. When I was sixteen, I visited the air force recruiter's booth at the Oklahoma State Fair. A man in a blue uniform asked me to tell him what numbers I could see in some circles filled with dots. I could see numbers in only four circles. He then told me that I was color-blind and would never fly airplanes in the air force.

I never had trouble seeing colors, and I had no problems the next few times that I took such tests. I had no trouble seeing the colors of lights and no problems with color chips. So what was the trouble with the dots in the circles? How could my color acuity vary? Easy—my eyes were very sensitive to color differences, and changes in lighting changed the colors I saw.

Once in Fairbanks, Alaska, I—along with nineteen men and four women—failed the color-blind test on our airman's medical. The FAA made us all take a Farnsworth lantern test for colors, and we all passed the test. What went wrong? The light bulb in the machine that projected the dots and circles had burned out. It had then been replaced with one of a slightly different color. Someone with a medical degree should have realized that something was wrong when one color-blind woman showed up, much less four in a population of less than sixty thousand people.

Most of my professional life had been involved with the interpretation of aerial photographs and satellite imagery. Therefore, I spent an immense amount of time studying and researching vision, stereo vision, and color vision.

The visible part of the electromagnetic spectrum can be split into several discrete frequencies that our brain assigns color values to. These discrete frequencies have no intrinsic color values of their own. Color and stereo visions are illusions generated in our brains. Scary, is it not? The question is, what else is just an illusion in our brains?

Boys are hardwired to be investigative scientists. This directed form of curiosity comes from the very core of their genetic code. They naturally begin to experiment with things at an early age. Boys stand in awe of the education that is derived from observing action and the resultant reaction. The unfortunate thing is that their sincere attempts at scientific experiments are erroneously regarded as mischief by women.

Those who think little boys are mean misinterpret their objectives. In particular, their actions are often considered as mischievous or cruel by their mothers, sisters, and the girl next door.

My mother was the middle child of a family of three girls. Therefore, she had very little experience as she grew up dealing with boys. Mother's oldest sister considered little boys to be dirty, smelly, and noisy things who, at best, should be kept in a pen behind the house. Throughout her teen years, my aunt spent a lot of effort protecting her baby sisters from such filthy little vermin. Obviously, this aunt never married.

As you can tell, Mother had mostly lived a female-oriented life until she fell in love with Dad. Fortunately for my brothers and me, when Mom met Dad, her hormones overrode the teachings of her spinster sister. Mother's dealings with little boys really began when she had me. I received two more brothers before she called a halt to the size of our family.

When I was four, Mother would start preparing my father's supper near the middle of the afternoon. One afternoon, after she had started getting things ready in the kitchen, I asked if I could cook the cat. To which she replied, "Sure, whatever!" My request was generated by the innate little boy concept that any definitive action will result in an unexpected but highly anticipated and entertaining reaction.

Mother was very good at working herself into a dither over most any task that she undertook. A characteristic that, I realized later in life, she had inherited from her mother. Nonetheless, she was distracted with the preparations of our evening meal and failed to connect what I had requested with the fact that she had lit the oven. She had done so in order to preheat the oven to the necessary temperature for whatever she was planning to cook.

Mom left the kitchen for some reason, and during her absence, my younger brother, Kib, and I finally trapped the cat and popped it into the oven. We sat down on the cool linoleum floor in front of the stove and were highly entertained by the actions of a panic-stricken cat. When Mother returned, she asked, "What's that I smell burning?" I pointed to the oven and innocently replied, "The cat."

Mother screamed and opened the oven door. The cat left the oven in one airborne leap to the kitchen sink with a flaming tail and a trail of smoke. Then in another single bound, he leapt out the open kitchen window that was over the sink. The cat's fate is unknown because he never came back.

Please keep in mind that I had asked, and Mother had given me permission to cook the cat. But this seemed to have very little bearing on Mother's rage, which lasted until—well, after Dad got home. However, this does emphasize the problems faced by a curious, well-meaning, young scientist.

An observation which might be unrelated to this event was that we never had another cat. However, the void wasn't noticed because I had two little brothers and several dogs to fulfill various roles in educational action-and-reaction experiments. It was a boost to my education when I discovered that, usually, dogs would willingly go where no little brother or cat would tread.

It was about this age that I discovered electricity. I remembered the event very clearly. It was an extremely positive learning experience. I very carefully stuck the two ends of a hairpin into the two thin slots molded in black Bakelite at the end of an extension cord. There was a flash of sparks and a jolt that knocked me backward into the middle of the room. The smoking hairpin had gone flying across the room, hitting the far wall with a loud snap. This had been so tremulously educational that I attempted to entice my baby brother to repeat the experiment. Unfortunately, his observational abilities had become highly developed by age two. He was not about to do to himself what he had just seen happen to me.

My mother and grandmother taught me to read at the age of four. By the time I was five, I would often read aloud the comic page from a recent newspaper to my grandfather. It was not unusual for me to read certain cartoon strips two or three times just to make sure that he and I understood what was being implied.

Perhaps it seemed strange that a skinny five-year-old boy would read to his grandfather this way, but Claude B. Cannon could neither read nor write. Even though I was what he considered as the runt of the litter, my pipe-smoking grandfather told me something that has given me confidence in myself all my life. Grandfather told me, "Because you can read, you're a keeper."

I have been diagnosed as a hopeless bibliophile by experts—other bibliophiles. As a child, I read everything that had letters on it. On Saturday mornings back in the 1940s, I would ride the bus to a nearby large town with my grandmother. We'd go to the big Carnegie Library and return two bags of well-read books and then check out two more bags of books for the next week's reading. The bad part was that they wouldn't let me check out the encyclopedias. Therefore, on Saturday afternoons while Grandmother shopped, I would sit in the library reading room, devouring volume after volume of various encyclopedias. Obviously, Grandmother was partly responsible for my incurable love of reading.

This affliction to reading might seem as a harmless activity for a young boy, but it did, on one occasion, cause considerable stress to my parents and the local school. When I was thirteen, a group of strange people from the University of Oklahoma came and gave every student a battery of tests on a great range of material from math and science to English and history. These tests had been developed by some group in Iowa and had taken four days of school time. The tests were timed, and I was always the first one to finish. I loved taking the tests because they involved reading. In particular, I liked where you read a paragraph and then answered questions about what you had read or used the data to solve a problem.

Six weeks after the tests, the strange university people returned to the school and berated the principal for allowing a bogus student to take the tests. The principal was pretty much of a jellyfish and would never have thought of doing anything that was disruptive or off line. He was upset at their accusations that a college senior with an IQ of 156 had been included in the testing body. I'm sure his first thought was that the football coach had pulled another of his outrageous stunts.

The university people demanded to meet student number T-158. The principal dug through his name-to-number list and came up with me.

I was called into the principal's office and grilled by the strange people for nearly an hour. I had no idea what was going on, but digging for information was fun. And as they would ask me questions about the tests, what I did at home for fun, and where I got my information, I fired questions back at them about things on the tests and ideas on rocket fuel. They were very poor at answering my questions. After a while, I think they got embarrassed that they couldn't answer my questions and sent me back to class.

Three days later, my parents were summoned to an evening school-board meeting by the principal. Not being told the reason for the summons before the meeting, Mother had worked herself into one of her classic dithers. Her parting line to me that night as they left for the meeting was "If you have embarrassed us in front of the school board, we're shipping you to St. Gregory's. There, the fathers will teach you some discipline." I didn't know what to think; I had no idea what was going on.

Later that evening when they returned, Dad had a huge grin on his face. Mother looked as if she had been crying. She gave me a big hug and, without a word, went to bed. Dad and I stayed up for another two hours, talking about the test results. He pointed out that my scores had skewed the results for the university people, and they dropped my scores from the overall data. He further pointed out that my avid reading had given me a big advantage over the other students. This just proved what he said he had known all along—that reading was the key to intelligence. He made a big point to me about not telling the other students because it might embarrass them. He also made it plain that if I did embarrass the other students, they would have to send me to St. Gregory's.

St. Gregory's was a Catholic boys' school in a nearby town that was known for its very strict discipline. In other words, it was where they sent the problem boys. They made it sound like jail. Thirty-five years later, I found myself teaching science and math at St. Gregory's. If they had sent me there when I was thirteen, I think I would have loved it.

My abilities as a chemist were in great demand in high school. I could make stink bombs, real bombs, high-octane racing fuel, moonshine, and potions. Sometimes, I made minor mistakes that were truly my fault. The worst was the time I blew myself up trying to set off a bomb outside the principal's office. A minor miscalculation cost me my letter jacket and a pair of blue jeans. The letter jacket probably saved my life. The humiliation that the principal heaped upon me was terrible. He laughed for two weeks. Between fits of laughter, he said, "I ought to beat you to death, but I think you got what you deserve." The man was absolutely heartless.

Actually, this was a great learning experience. It had not been my idea to bomb the principal's office. I was only fifteen at the time, and when three seniors told me how cool it would be to scare the principal in such a manner, I swallowed their line. They smoothly convinced me that such an event would make a geek like me immensely popular with everyone, especially with the girls. For weeks after this event, everyone avoided me as if I was about to detonate at any moment. For a brief period here, I had the fabulous nickname of "The Mad Bomber"! Needless to say, my popularity with the girls did not improve.

Most importantly, I learned that humidity influences the rate of some chemical reactions. The development of my time-delayed fuse of glycerin and potassium permanganate had been in a comfortable dry lab that I had built in the attic of the garage. It had been raining the day of the bombing, and the potassium permanganate had soaked up a little moisture from the damp air on the trip from my lab to the school, thus accelerating the reaction of my time-delayed fuse. I also learned that when one is at the heart of such an explosion, you don't hear a great big boom. You are only aware of a giant shock wave, which ripples through your body at the speed of sound.

The high school faculty was mostly sickos of some type. They had to be or they could have gotten a better job at another school. The worst teacher was the band instructor. He thought he was wonderful; and to prove it, he attempted to save us "scum" (as he called us) from ourselves. After a major verbal attempt by him to alter my feelings about my flattop haircut and my black leather jacket, I struck back. I shoved a potato up the tailpipe of his new 1957 Plymouth. I shoved it as far as I could with a broomstick. The car would start. It would go about one hundred feet, and then it would die. Attempts to restart the car would be to no avail unless you let the car set for about an hour or more. Then it would start, run for a few seconds, and then die again. It went through this cycle over and over again—first, in the school's parking lot, and then for the rest of the week, in various mechanic shops across town. During that time, the band teacher lost a lot of hair and became hated by every mechanic in town. I think it was the shop teacher who finally figured out what the problem was and fixed it. There was a moral to this story. The band teacher had insulted and abused so many people that he didn't know where to begin with accusations. He solved our problem. He quit and became a problem for another school.

There is a very fine line between a properly functioning solid-propellant rocket and a bomb. I had perfected the chemistry of a solid-propellant rocket by the time I was sixteen. However, the process had not been without its trials. Numerous craters across our pasture attested to the exhaustion of a rocket's entire fuel supply within ten nanoseconds after ignition. It had taken me nearly three months to discover a mixture of fertilizer, sulfur, charcoal, and chicken manure, which would give a burn rate just short of an instant detonation.

This mixture provided plenty of lift for a rocket, accompanied with the desired amount of yellow flame and huge clouds of brown smoke. The area immediately downwind of a rocket liftoff was declared off limits to humans and cows. I assumed all rocket launch sites were plagued with this problem of a short-lived, downwind, dead zone.

Launching a sizable payload had been the easy part. Returning that which had been launched in less than a highly compressed or extremely fragmented condition was a real challenge. I was an avid reader of such scientific journals as *Popular Science* and *Boy's Life*. When the headlines disclosed that the fastest man on Earth was an air force flight surgeon on a rocket-powered sled, I thought, *I can do that*. The main purpose for his rapid ride was to test a parachute for the safe return to Earth of a hapless pilot. I further thought, *Shucks, NASA and the air force aren't too far ahead of me*. In fact, we seemed to be nearly neck and neck in the race for space.

In less than two days, I had attached my space capsule to a farm-made rocket sled. My space capsule was a converted thirty-two-gallon stainless-steel cream separator. This gave me a steel cylinder with a conical end. It looked as streamlined as a Fourth of July skyrocket. I had removed the draw-off valve from the conical end (formerly the bottom) in order to provide for an enhanced flow of cool air to the astronaut. The capsule had a narrow window down the side of the conical end (previously used to judge the milk/cream interface) for the astronaut to view the forthcoming conditions of his flight.

The rocket sled consisted of the angle iron from several discarded bed frames and eight mower wheels. Well, it may have been more of a wagon than a sled, but the semantics aren't important. Besides, I was sure that the air force would have used wheels if such had been available to them. I was proud of the fact that all eight wheels had the same diameter, although two of the wheels were on a very short time loan from Dad's new mower. I had built a rectangular boxlike frame and a cradle for the space capsule out of the angle iron. The four wheels were bolted to a side down the length of the box. I'm suspicious that someone saw my rocket sled and later used the concept for the truck-type landing gear of a Boeing 747.

The one thing that a farm of the fifties was never short of was baling wire. I attached the capsule and rocket motor to the sled or wagon with several hundred turns of baling wire. I fully expected men to travel to Mars with several hundred feet of baling wire. What else was there for emergency tie down? Later, when duct tape became available, I knew baling wire was in trouble.

My new parachute consisted of a cluster of several smaller chutes. The pack for the chutes was attached to the upper edge on the rear of the space capsule, in front of the rocket motor. In this technology, I was way ahead of NASA. They had their share of disasters before they fixed the Apollo spacecraft with a chute cluster instead of one giant chute. The reason for NASA's slow development was that it took a while for some of my mother's kindergarten graduates to filter into the system.

Two days after I had read about Dr. Griener's rocket-sled ride, I was looking down a smoothly graded path to the biggest pond on the farm. At the beginning of the path sat the space capsule attached to a short-stack rocket motor. This complete unit was lashed with the baling wire to my eight-wheeled dolly. The concept was simple, the rocket motor would take the space capsule and dolly up to speed just short of the pond. At that point, the parachute cluster would open and bring the whole flaming mess to a stop at the edge of the pond. The pond was just for backup. If the chutes failed, then the space capsule and the eight-wheeled dolly would splash to a stop in the water, not too unlike the air force's rocket sled.

A bad thing about those days was that I had no camera for a documentation unit. The only documentation unit I had was Tim. Fortunately, he was at the center of things. Surely, everyone used their siblings for experiments.

I stood at the end of two long wires and ignited the rocket motor. Flame and smoke engulfed the vehicle. There was an unearthly, ear-piercing screech, and the space capsule plus propulsion unit slipped through the baling-wire bindings like it had been lubricated with a mixture of pig snot and calf slobbers. This was one of my early lessons about inertia and friction.

The entire unit traveled through the air and down the path just about the radius of a mower wheel above the ground. It hit the water, and much to my amazement, it ricocheted like a flat-sided rock off the water and back into the air. At that point, the parachute cluster deployed. The asymmetrical drag of the chutes attached to just the upper edge at the rear of the space capsule lifted the unit to a departure angle somewhat greater than the original angle of incidence. An angle which aimed the smoking unit with the trailing cluster of chutes into the willow trees on the far side of the pond.

I had one of those fleeting moments of insight. There was obviously more to using a track for this experiment than just a lack of wheels.

Due to its aerodynamic shape, the space capsule easily penetrated the foliage of the willow trees. However, the trailing cluster of chutes tangled with the tree branches like satin with rose thorns. The space capsule was brought up short, and it made two very rapid three-hundred-sixty-degree turns to the left. Having come to the end of its rope, the capsule tightly wedged itself between the rope and several small branches. The willow trees looked similar to something I would see lots of later in life: a long-haired hippie with a very tight headband.

I ran around the pond dam and climbed the willow trees, which had been bound up like a shock of wheat. I cut the space capsule free of the rope and the tree limbs with my scout knife. With a solid thud, it hit the mud beneath the trees. I jumped out of the trees and unscrewed the wing nuts on the door that I had made in the side of the cream separator. Tim, covered with the kapok fibers from a war surplus life preserver, exploded from the interior.

"Damn it, Flattop! The parachute didn't work!"

"Sure it did! There was a minor malfunction back at the start, and it messed up the timing of events."

He looked pale. He gasped for breath and made a small retching sound.

"Hold it, Tim!" I yelled with my hands in front of me, to ward off the evil. "I just saw Mom and Mother Bell drive up." He swallowed and began taking forced breaths.

Belva—nicknamed Mother Bell—was my mother's mother. She had one old-fashioned cure for everything. Whether you were heaving or bleeding, she felt you should get a clean start toward the process of healing with an enema. Tim would rather suffer a great list of discomforts than let his grandmother give him an enema. He was rapidly beginning to improve.

He took two more deep breaths and exclaimed, "Flattop, if I ever get to Mars, I ain't coming back!"

His declaration surprised me. "Why is that, baby brother?"

"I think the return trip would be too dangerous."

Later, after much training in physics and the forces of gravity, I had to agree with him. It's amazing how astute a six-year-old can be.

My senior year in high school can be easily summed up—so many girls, so little time. High school itself offered me absolutely no challenge, but girls were a big challenge. I learned quickly that if one was going to exploit the charms of more than one girl at a time, they couldn't be at the same school, or they couldn't be in the same town. The reason for this mutual-exclusion phenomenon was the girl-girl network. This network was the main reason teenage girls dated boys. It gave them something to talk about. It appeared that teenage girls in the same town spent a lot of time comparing their boyfriends.

My friend Larry and I made a great discovery at church camp. Usually, girls never lowered themselves to talk to girls from another town. This discovery opened up a whole new world of women to us teenage men. This might be related to the nautical term "a girl in every port."

The only limiting factor in our new world was the geographical distance that could be covered in one night. Teenage boys suffered from some restraints, such as being at work the next morning. Gasoline was seventeen cents a gallon, so it was not a big problem if you had a part-time job. Larry and I both had part-time jobs, but they were daytime jobs. Therefore, we had the entire night to play geographical girls. Sleep? I can't remember sleeping between the ages of sixteen and twenty-one. If I slept during that time, I'm sure it was because I passed out from exhaustion. That might explain why I don't remember it. I remember waking up in some strange places—like under a car or in a ditch. But I don't remember getting ready to go to bed some place for the sole purpose of sleeping.

My part-time job was with a motor parts company. This gave me an edge in the game because I could get engine parts cheap, and I had access to a machine shop. This was one of the reasons I don't think I slept during those years. If I wasn't in that shop at night, hopping up my car, I was playing geographical girls.

Playing geographical girls was not easy, and it could be dangerous from several points of view. The most difficult part was the timing. This meant scheduling your dates in order to minimize the travel time in one evening. The best approach was to make a large circle—which put you through a couple of towns in one evening, and you could return home before sunrise. It helps, of course, to have a fast car. I even repainted my car every other week. In this manner, I didn't leave much of a pattern that could be noticed.

While you're making the circuit, the local girlfriend thinks you've been working on your car all night, and she has spent the night talking about you with her girlfriends. I later learned that this was a poor assumption on my part. She—like the girls that I'd been dating in the other towns—was playing geographical boys. Unaware of this, Larry and I were living our delusion with zest, and we were loving it.

Larry came up with a peculiar problem one day. He needed to appear sick enough to get out of school so he could spend the day on a lake with one of his geographical girls. Getting out of school was no problem for her. It seemed that when a girl says she's sick, no one questions it unless she has overused the excuse. However, if a boy claimed he was sick, he better be near death before they would cut him any slack at all. Well, there was Larry's problem. Since I was the local chemist, he laid the problem at my feet. They say "a friend in need is a thing to heed." When you're in high school, a friend in need was indeed a thing to heed. You never knew when you were going to be on the needy end.

On the morning of the fateful day in the school parking lot, I had him eat half a loaf of white bread, down a bottle of aspirins, and wash it all down with a double cola. Then I told him to dash the fifty yards to the principal's office, and nature would make him a convincing sight. I may have overdone the prescription a little. When Larry entered the principal's office, he erupted great gobs of white stuff and passed out. I didn't know I had done such a great job until the ambulance drove up. They kept him in the hospital under observation all day. Needless to say, he missed his date on the lake. I later convinced him it was all his fault because he hadn't told me he had such a sensitive stomach.

Well, it seems that things go wrong when you give good ideas to dumb people. One of my geographical girls had a request similar to Larry's. I gave her one of my milder sickness potions with strict instructions. I told her to break up an Alka-Seltzer tablet and coat the pieces with chocolate. Then swallow them and drink a warm coke. This produces a mild gaseous eruption with positive results. The potion worked fine. She was pleased, and so was I. We had a great time in the city that day. It was later that week that disaster struck. She shared the secret formula with a girlfriend who figured if one was good, then four tablets ought to be better. It must have been quite a sight. It was reported that she produced frothy brown fluid from every opening in her face.

The bad part was, my geographical girl revealed her source of information. Instead of dying a horrible death to protect her friend, she squealed like a stuck pig. New rule: never trust a girl with sensitive information. I crossed that geographical girl off my map and repainted my car.

I don't know why Larry had so much trouble with women in high school—bad taste maybe. Larry had the ability to make his problems my problems. A dark-eyed little Susie in another town wanted to maintain a relationship with him, but her father was absolutely opposed to such a relationship. In other words, the man hated Larry's guts. Since my mother was a schoolteacher, I had her old man's approval. What good it did that my mother was a schoolteacher, I never understood. In my case, I don't think my mother would have understood it either.

Being incredibly resourceful, Larry and I solved the problem. I would swing by and pick Susie up in my car early in the evening. I would deliver her to Larry at the Hamburger King and then go pick up my date. About midnight, I would rendezvous with Larry again. I would leave my date with him, if I still had one, and take Susie home. Larry soon got tired of this and found a new love that was fatherless, which disappointed Susie and me greatly. We were enjoying some hot good-night kisses on her front porch just to keep her father convinced of the relationship. I wisely never told Larry of this sacrifice.

It was the fall of 1958. The new Buick Wildcat convertibles were out. They and the people in them looked great. I, being a freshman in college, knew that I would soon have a degree and would be rich. It was only logical that I should be considering what kind of new wheels I would soon buy.

During my first day at college, the chemistry teacher asked where my slide rule was. *My what?* I had to buy a device composed of three sticks that could multiply and divide. Now I could already multiply and divide. What I needed was a set of sticks like this that could spell or do that grammar thing.

The real shock of college wasn't the classes or the food. Hey, I survived two summers of forest camp. I knew about bad food, birds, bugs, bees, and trees. Once you've seen a film about what rabbits do in the bush, you think you've seen it all.

The real life-threatening shock was the city girls. They were strange-talking, catlike creatures in flimsy clothes. When they said words like "I want more," they meant money, not ice cream.

Country girls I knew something about. Not a lot, or as much as I wanted to know, but enough that we could talk about life's major problems—world-shaking problems like tractors, horses, moonshine, and fat-stock shows. Country girls knew their way to the feed store and back by themselves. The city girls didn't seem to know where anything was, not even where they lived.

Dating city girls was a real education. They had no idea how to drive a pickup truck, but they could hot-wire a car. They even had this weird notion you could go swimming and not get your hair wet. Stranger yet, they came connected to a telephone. It was some sort of an umbilical cord that fed them life-sustaining substances.

Being curious and vitamin deficient, I opted to date a few. I asked one lovely feline-looking thing if she wanted to go look at the stars with me one evening. She seemed quite anxious to do such a thing. I parked my hopped-up Chevy coupe on top of a hill south of town, and she purred, "This is nice." I said, "Baby, you ain't seen nothing yet." I got out of the car, opened the trunk, and got my big telescope out. She got out of the car, took a look at the telescope, and said, "God —— you weren't —— kidding were you." City girls have a way with words that could peel paint.

It was my second year at college when I met Joyce, the all-natural girl. When she was fourteen, her parents pulled her out of a tree, put shoes on her, and sent her to school in the city. Joyce had gotten the well-rounded education you hear so much talk about. Joyce could drive a tractor, worm pigs, and make a sheriff's deputy blush with her language. Her hair was just her hair. She never took the time to do things to her hair like the city girls. She wore the flimsy city-girl clothes, but not the shoes. Joyce made a compromise there. She carried those shoes everywhere she went. Like some women with their car keys, she was always leaving them somewhere that she couldn't remember. We would spend half the weekend looking for her shoes.

I ran cross-country track in high school and college. I was reasonably fast on my feet. However, Joyce could outrun me. There was no chasing Joyce; if she was leaving, she was gone like a cool breeze. This really impressed me. The only other woman to outrun me was my mother. My mother was always chasing me, but it wasn't like the times I was chasing Joyce. I might be the reason that my mother always stayed in such good shape without aerobics or any other exercise.

My Chevy coupe burned up on reentry one night, so I acquired another set of wheels. Since I couldn't afford the new 1959 Buick yet, I had gotten the next best thing: a three-ton 1949 Buick. It was a green four-door sedan shaped like a tank. That was a real party car. We could get six couples in it on Saturday night and still have room to dance in the back.

Well, Joyce and I pretty much lived in that old Buick until summer. Then her parents got a strange idea that Joyce ought to see California at its prime. It was part of their idea of a well-rounded education, no doubt. She discovered that there was a new subculture of people like her in California. They were called beatniks, or hippies. Joyce, the all-natural girl, didn't come back. She remained there with the "what you see is what you get" crowd. The last time I saw her was in San Francisco, eighteen years ago. She still looked about like she did back in those college days. Her hair was untamed, and she was still carrying her shoes.

The Moon Program

In addition to wanting to be a pilot, I did wish to be an astronomer. By the time I was fourteen, I was a book-smart astronomer. I had read everything I could find on the subject and could discuss what was known about the planets with anyone.

When I was sixteen, I ground and polished a six-inch mirror for a reflecting telescope. My father helped me get the mirror blank aluminized and found me a five-foot-long piece of aluminum irrigation pipe. Using galvanized pipe for an equatorial mount, I assembled a very good telescope. The first time that I looked through a telescope and saw the craters on the moon, the rings of Saturn, and the moons of Jupiter was with a telescope that I had built. I still have and use that telescope.

I spent the first two and one half years of college making up high school deficiencies. The high school I had attended offered no science, math, foreign languages, or real English classes. I had to start at the bottom in all these subjects. However, my desire to be a scientist was so intense that I persevered.

Upon completion of my deficiencies, I immediately declared my major in astronomy. On the first semester, I took a course in astronomy and a course in geology. I was shocked to discover that astronomers were interested in stars but not planets. Obviously, geologists were interested in planets (at least one planet) very intensely. Before the next semester began, I defected from astronomy and majored in geology. At that time, geology was in an economic downturn, and everyone told me I was making a bad mistake. It turned out it was the best mistake I ever made.

Four years later, I graduated with a master's degree in geology and went to work as an astrogeologist in the Apollo Moon Program.

NASA's Center of Astrogeology was located in Flagstaff, Arizona. I had arrived at my intellectual heaven. Dr. Gene Shoemaker, the father of astrogeology, was the director of the center. He started off my career here with a field trip to Meteor Crater, Arizona, in the company of seven Apollo astronaut candidates. It was so intimidating that I could hardly talk. Throughout this early part of my professional career, I was always the youngest in any group by ten years.

For the two years that I worked on my master's degree, I worked for the Oklahoma Geological Survey as an aerial photograph interpretation specialist and geologic mapper. These two abilities were the keys to my employment at the Center of Astrogeology.

As soon as I arrived at the Center of Astrogeology, I was assigned lunar mapping projects. Under the tutelage of Dr. Dave Roddy, I quickly learned the key geomorphic features that were critical to a useful map of the moon. The navigability of the lunar surface was a top priority for future sampling and exploration of the moon. The smoothest areas were to be carefully noted and located as they would be the first chosen for vehicle-landing sites. The areas containing large chunks of ejecta were labeled as boulder patches. These would be impossible areas to safely land and were to be avoided at all costs.

The Ranger series of lunar probes showed the lunar surface to be heavily cratered up to the point they crashed. Dr. Shoemaker had correctly predicted what the lunar surface looked like, as had several other geologists. The moon's surface had been pounded with meteorites of all sizes for billions of years, creating a surface that resulted from being cratered and recratered.

Astronomer Thomas Gold predicted the lunar surface would be covered with powdery dust hundreds of feet thick. Carl Sagan predicted that the lunar surface would be hard and smooth, consisting of cold lava flows. Both were wrong because they knew practically no geology at all. But they got the media's attention and caused the moon program grief throughout its history because they were geologically illiterate.

I had been picked to map the landing site for *Apollo 12*, which was located on the north shore of Mare Cognitum, just below the moon's equator. *Ranger 7* had previously impacted near there and provided me with high-resolution photographs of the site. Then *Surveyor 3* landed in the site during April 1967 and dug around in the regolith, providing information on the stability of the surface. One month later, *Lunar*

Orbiter 4 flew over the site and photographed *Surveyor 3* sitting on the rim of an old degraded crater. This was the data set that I had to use for mapping.

You cannot know the feeling I received, seeing the *Surveyor 3* sitting on the surface in the photographs taken by *Lunar Orbiter 4*. The resolution of the *Orbiter 4* photographs was better than one meter.

At the conclusion of the Orbiter program, we had a conference at the Center of Astrogeology to sum up the results. They had built six Lunar Orbiter spacecraft in hopes that at least three would work. The first five worked perfectly, giving us photography of nearly the entire moon. The question came up: what to do with *Orbiter 6*?

The first suggestion was to send it to Mars. Well, we didn't have a vehicle big enough to send it to Mars. So I stood up and said, "Let's put it in Earth's orbit." I quickly got a very loud response. I was told to "shut up and to never mention that option again." Then Gene Shoemaker stood up and invited me to his office immediately.

You have to realize I was using photography that had better than a one-meter resolution that had been taken by a spacecraft in orbit about another planet. I had no access to orbital imagery of Earth that was better than twenty meters in resolution. At that time, the official lie was that we did not have the technology to do better resolution than that. When you know that there is something out there that's better than what you have in your hand, it's difficult to be happy.

In order to train astronauts how to make meaningful sample selections and to test lunar roving vehicles, Gene Shoemaker had us create an area of craters in a cinder field east of Flagstaff, Arizona, that resembled the *Apollo 12* landing site. He named it Mare Incognitum.

We used a small mountain of fertilizer and diesel fuel to create Mare Incognitum. However, I was already a famous bomb maker, and I felt right at home in this endeavor. Blowing holes in the cinder field was great fun, but the best part was yet to come.

One week had been set aside to test possible lunar rovers. Trucks arrived on Monday and off-loaded approximately twenty possible rover candidates. One was the size of a medium-sized RV on large tractor-type tires. As soon as its right front wheel bounced into a small crater, the vehicle rolled on its side and lay there helpless. A smaller two-man vehicle drove into a crater twelve feet deep and disappeared. The unconsolidated cinders made the crater into a giant ant-lion trap. The more the vehicle struggled, the deeper it became buried.

It was a disastrous week. No one was more disappointed than the astronauts who felt that they were doomed to do a lot of walking on the moon. By Friday, the wrecked and battered vehicles had been hauled away. It was a gloomy weekend in Flagstaff.

On Monday morning, as I got out of my '55 Pontiac in the parking lot, Dave Roddy roared up in his pickup and yelled, "Quick, get in, we have to go see what has happened at Mare Incognitum!" Dave didn't seem to know what had happened at the old cinder field other than Gene Shoemaker wanted us there fast. We had been at the same party Saturday night, and Dave had not been more morose than anyone else. I was baffled at what had occurred.

When we arrived, there was a crowd of people from the center standing on the edge of Mare Incognitum, looking across the cratered terrain. Dave drove beside the crowd and stopped. We were shocked! Tire tracks from some mystery vehicle ran across the entire area. The tracks went into and out of each crater, even the one that was twenty-five feet deep and the ant lion den. Someone had technology that was better than what Boeing and General Motors had developed.

On the weekend, some young people from Flagstaff had brought their homemade dune buggies to Mare Incognitum and had conquered it all. Now you know why the real lunar rovers resembled scaled-down dune buggies.

Being part of mission control at the Manned Spacecraft Center in Houston, Texas, during the *Apollo 12* mission could have been the height of most of anyone's professional career. This was just the second moon landing, and the excitement at the center was infectious. My reason for being there was just in case the astronauts had any questions about the map that I had made for them. Just how many geologists could say that a map that he had made was used on another planet? I think there were just five of us. *Apollo 11* forgot their map.

I often tell people that reality was stranger than fiction. Not a single science-fiction writer predicted that when men went to the moon, the eyes of the whole world would go with them. It had been assumed that the television routine for *Apollo 12* would go the same as it had for *Apollo 11*, but that was not to be. At the beginning of the surface excursion, the camera was pointed at the sun, and the imaging tube was overloaded with photons and ceased to function. This was disappointing at the time, but overall, the mission was a great success. The crew walked over to the *Surveyor 3* spacecraft—the very one that I could see on the *Orbiter 4* imagery—and cut off some choice pieces like its TV camera and returned them to Earth for study.

After this mission, it felt that going to the moon was a walk in the park. Of course, *Apollo 13* brought us all back to reality. Nonetheless, there was talk among the astrogeologists about where to go from here. What I wanted was to be part of *Apollo 22* and visit Rupes Recta, the Straight Wall. It's the face of a large fault nearly a hundred miles long and a thousand feet high. It would be an awesome view into the mysteries of the moon. My second choice would be *Apollo 30* to the lunar far side.

But the Democratic Congress needed money for its social programs, and the word came down that *Apollo 17* would be the last. The Apollo program had been mostly about politics and very little about science.

By the time of *Apollo 14*, NASA became very interested in satellites for Earth observation. Since I was a geologist that could fluently read and speak physics, NASA stuck me in the early part of the Landsat program, when it was referred to as ERTS. Since it was about building and launching satellites for Earth resources, I was, of course, very interested. Earth being one of my favorite planets, I was extremely keen on learning more about it. This put me on a career path that launched me into a teaching position at the University of Alaska in Fairbanks, Alaska, and eventually, into independent consulting work on a global scale.

One of the perks of living and working in Flagstaff, Arizona, was its location. It was just seventy-two miles from the Grand Canyon, a holy place for geologists. Walking down into the canyon to the Colorado River, you travel nearly a mile through the Earth's crust. I have made several trips into the Grand Canyon at different places. The following story is of my most memorable.

A Short Hike in the Grand Canyon

Day One

On Sunday, August 25, 1968, at 8:00 a.m., I descended into the eastern end of the Grand Canyon on the Tanner Trail. This easternmost trail was not maintained by the National Park Service, and therefore, its condition was unknown. The heavy rains earlier this summer had washed away the trail for the first two miles, and I had to lower myself and pack with a rope on several occasions. The Tanner Trail, for the most part, is not steep—but the gentle gradient makes the trip one of the longest in the canyon. It is about eighteen miles long and, in some places, runs along narrow ledges less than a foot wide.

I was dismayed at the amount of abandoned camping gear, such as sleeping bags and cookware, which littered the trail. It appeared that people attempting to walk out up the trail would tire of their gear and just toss it rather than haul it to the top. Some of it was so deteriorated, it must have been there for years.

There's an entertaining variety of rocks along the first few miles of the trail. I stopped to rest at the point where the Redwall Limestone is on top of the Temple Butte Limestone. There is an unconformity at this point where several million years of geologic time were not represented. There had been rocks deposited in this time interval, but here, they had been eroded away before the deposition of the Redwall Limestone. To me, the most awesome aspect about the Grand Canyon was not the hundreds of millions of years of time that were represented by the rocks that were in the canyon walls, but the even greater amount of geologic time that wasn't represented in the vertical mile of rocks. Therefore, unconformities hold a special fascination for me. They were ancient landscapes where geomorphic process raged, eroding away the rocks that had been laid down during a previous time. I always wonder what it must have been like on that ancient surface of Earth when the stars were in different positions in the sky.

While resting, I spotted a bright piece of rock protruding from the unconformity. I dug out a beautiful white crystalline mass as large as my hand. It was much heavier than the limestone above and below it. They were two crystals that had intergrown into each other. This was referred to as a penetration twin and was a diagnostic characteristic of some minerals. I had seen identical specimens of this mineral in the lab; it was barite. It weighed about two pounds, but I wasn't about to carry an extra two pounds on this trip. I laid it down about twenty feet off the trail near the unconformity. I suppose it's still lying there.

The last one-third of the Tanner Trail was through the red Dox Sandstone of late Precambrian age. It's a boring, silty sandstone more than 650 million years old. Most of my trip along the river would be in the gorge that the Colorado River has cut in this rock.

I arrived at the Colorado River just below the Tanner Canyon Rapids after nine hours of hiking at 5:00 p.m. I had averaged two miles an hour in the heat, carrying a heavy pack. There was no source of water along the trail, and after eighteen miles of rough desert, the river sure looked cool and inviting. I dropped my pack, removed my clothes, and waded in; it felt wonderful.

I found a large flat rock to sleep on that night; but first, I had to battle a rattlesnake for it. He quickly fled from the menacing blows of my walking stick. I put my air mattress and sleeping bag on it and fell asleep before I could see stars in the early evening sky. I did notice some thunderstorms off to the northeast. My thoughts were that they would continue on east throughout the evening and were of no concern to me.

Day Two

The next morning, Monday, August 26, I awoke at 5:30 a.m. to find a small green frog in my sleeping bag. Frogs are better than snakes any day. He probably got in my sleeping bag to hide from snakes. It was cool in the canyon, and the sun had not yet peaked over the rim. The gurgling and splashing of the Tanner Canyon Rapids sounded like an ancient music of the universe as I ate some breakfast and repacked my gear. Life doesn't get any better than this. You're young (I was twenty-seven), you're strong, the weather is beautiful, and adventure into the unknown lies just down the river.

I checked my maps and reviewed my plans. Before starting this trip, I found all the information I could about this part of the Grand Canyon. In 1955, a man named Colin Fletcher had walked along the Colorado River from the west to the east end of the canyon. He did not indicate that he had encountered any problems as he hiked through here from the Hance Trail to the Tanner Trail. He did his hiking naked. From my previous hiking experiences in the Grand Canyon, I had noted that what the bugs and snakes didn't bite, the thorns on the bushes pricked and scraped.

A math professor at NAU had told me he had taken this trip a few years ago, and it was not a difficult hike. He also recommended floating the smaller rapids on an air mattress. The topographic maps seemed to indicate that there was indeed a way along the Colorado River between these two trails. My plan was to travel along the river downstream from the bottom of the Tanner Trail to the Hance Trail. The distance between the two trails along the lower river channel was about nine miles. I had planned to spend today walking these nine miles, and then tomorrow, I would walk out of the canyon by way of the Hance Trail. It sounded easy.

I left my camp at the large flat rock at 6:30 a.m., heading west and south parallel to the river high on the south bank. By 9:30 a.m., I had traveled more than three and a half miles down the course of the river and found myself at a high shear wall in the Dox Sandstone that I couldn't scale or walk around. The south bank of the lower river channel here was a wall of red rock about fifteen hundred feet high, but the north bank was bordered with a broad sandbar. The river was about six hundred feet wide at this point and was flowing smoothly with no rapids.

I tied my pack to the air mattress, donned a life jacket, and pushed out into the river, swimming for the north bank. It was exhilarating being swept along the river as the ripples gently roiled the surface of the water. The river carried me nearly a mile before I was able to reach the sandbar on the north bank. It had carried me about twice as far as I had thought it would. I made a note of this. As fast as the river flowed, I had to make a strong effort to get across it before I was swept away from my intended objective and ended up in some bad rapids.

As I deflated the air mattress and made ready to walk along the north bank to a point below the rapids at Unkar Creek, two riverboats full of adventurous rafters floated past. They gave me a very hearty hello, which I returned in the same manner. (I noted that the time was 10:00 a.m.) The delta at the mouth of Unkar Creek was large, and as I cut across it, I walked upon some extensive Indian ruins. There were pottery shards and the foundations for dwellings scattered everywhere. I was surprised because books always insist that the Indians were afraid of the canyon and would never enter it. The ruins had obviously been dug into extensively. I picked up of some of the shards and was fascinated with the texture of woven straw that had been fired into them. Later, I discovered that Powel had noticed the ruins, and the myth had been generated by the Park Service to thwart anyone's possible interest in the canyon as a source of ruins and artifacts. It is obvious on the topographic maps that Unkar Creek would be an easy route to access the river from the North Rim. In fact, the Indians probably crossed the river near the Tanner Canyon Rapids during low water in the fall and winter.

The Unkar Rapids were rated as a level six on a scale of ten in relation to their force and difficulty. As I walked across the delta, I marveled at the force and energy being displayed by the river as it roared over the jumble of rocks. Trees disappeared into whirlpools, and huge standing waveforms shot debris deep into the channel. The debris and trees would pop up twenty or thirty yards downstream, battered and peeled of bark and limbs. It was an impressive display of the power of running water.

Rapids on most rivers are formed by resistant ledges or tilted layers of rocks. The rapids in the Grand Canyon are formed by massive piles of boulders that have been washed down the canyons of the side creeks by torrential floods. Therefore, the rapids are located at the mouths of the side creeks, and from there, they extend for a short ways downstream. The bigger the side creek is, the larger the pile of boulders at the mouth. Subsequently, the bigger rapids are created from a greater supply of boulders.

At 11:00 a.m., I had crossed the delta and was at a point where the river was bounded with high walls on both sides. There was one more set of rapids left before the river once again became a smooth ribbon of green. I reinflated the air mattress, affixed my gear to it, and entered the water. The rapids were small with standing waves of about three feet in amplitude.

For about 1,500 feet, I got quite a thrilling ride; then the water chute I was in shot me into a whirlpool that looked like it went to the center of the Earth. I, the air mattress, and my gear went down and around for over fifteen seconds. I held my breath and waited for the whirlpool to subside. As I was pulled down into the vortex, I was beaten with sticks and limbs. I was sucked deep enough down into the water that it got dark. The whirlpool spit me into the back eddy and slammed me into a rock ledge just upstream from the whirlpool. Before I could get a hold of something to use to pull myself out, the whirlpool grabbed me and took me down again. I had not expected this at all and did not have time to catch a full breath. I was struggling for breath when it again spit me into the back eddy. Coughing and choking for air, I just managed to catch a full breath before it took me down again. This time, when it spit me into the back eddy, I swam as hard as I could upstream. This got me out of the influence of the whirlpool, and I managed to go upstream to a point where I could grab on to a narrow rock ledge. I climbed onto the ledge very banged up and wet. Later, I saw similar-sized whirlpools take trees, twenty feet long, completely out of sight for fifteen to twenty seconds. Back on the north bank again, I rested on the narrow ledge for a while as I caught my breath. Thirty-eight years later, I can assure you that was the most scared I've been in my life.

After I caught my breath, I climbed along the ledge until I found a place where I could lower myself with my rope to a lower ledge. From this lower ledge, I climbed down to another sandbar on the north bank of the river.

I was still shaken from the experience with the whirlpool, but I had to cross the river because the north bank had now become an impasse of vertical rock, and there were no trails out of the canyon on this side of the river for several miles. The river here was wide and smooth but, nonetheless, flowing very fast.

After the whirlpool, the river looked mean and ugly regardless of its apparent state. I needed to get to the south bank because the trail out was over there. However, below this point were the small rapids at the mouth of Escalante Creek. immediately followed by the Nevills Rapids at the mouth of Seventy-five Mile Creek. The Nevills Rapids (named after Norman Nevills, an early river runner, who died in a small plane crash in 1949) are rated as level 10 rapids and considered as the worst of the rapids in the Grand Canyon.

As I sat and pondered my options, I noticed that the high-speed chute of the fastest flowing water near the center of the channel slowly oscillated from one side of the channel to the other with a period of about two minutes. If I got into the river, the high-speed chute could keep me on this side of the river until I wouldn't have time to make the south bank before throwing me into the next rapids. This was not a good situation. I sat and timed the oscillations, realizing that if I entered the river as the oscillation reached its maximum on the north side, I could ride the chute as it slowly shifted over to the south bank. This was one of those ingenious solutions you come up with when you're only twenty-seven years old.

With great trepidation, I again entered the river, swimming for all I was worth toward the south bank. What a ride, the water velocity in the high-speed chute must have been forty miles an hour. The far bank was whizzing by awfully fast. By the time I felt rocks on the south bank, the river had carried me nearly a mile downstream. However, I had managed to safely reach the south bank. As I sat on the rocks of the south bank, catching my breath, I could hear the rapids of Escalante Creek gurgling and chuckling about one half of a mile below me. I was surely thankful to be on the south bank.

It was 1:30 p.m., and I was less than two and one half miles from the Hance Trail. It looked like an easy open hike from here to it. I had survived the rapids; therefore, I felt certain that I would be able climb out on the Hance Trail tomorrow.

After half a mile of easy hiking along the sandbar on the south bank, I reached the delta of Escalante Creek. The topographic map indicated that I could walk from here to the Hance Trail along the south bank. I was pleased that I'd not seen any litter since I left the end of the Tanner Trail. This was turning into a walk in the park.

Eager to reach the bottom of the Hance Trail, I didn't even stop to rest at the delta of Escalante Creek. You cannot imagine my shock about thirty minutes later when I discovered that the path along the river indicated by the map was under about ten feet of water. I now realized that the river was a lot higher than usual.

The rapids were rough here at the mouth of Escalante Creek, indeed, as rough or as worse than any of the rapids I'd seen upstream. I was still shaken by my experience with the Unkar Rapids, so I tried to climb out along a ledge that ran above Seventy-Five Mile Creek. With no such luck, I ran into sheer cliffs that I couldn't climb. From my vantage point, I could see the Nevills Rapids. I was astounded at the raging torrent of water boiling through those rapids.

I tried to climb out Escalante Creek with the thought that I could either continue to the Hance Trail at a higher elevation or return to the Tanner Trail. The walls of Escalante Creek were also beyond my abilities to scale. I couldn't climb or walk out; the river was the only choice. Looking up from the end of the small-boxed canyon that I was in, I could see a wild goat looking down at me from the top of the cliff. He seemed as surprised to see me as I was to see him. I yelled, and he disappeared from the top of the cliff. No doubt, he was going to tell his buddies what he'd just seen.

The rapids at Escalante Creek had four-foot high-standing waves in them. Where the Escalante Creek rapids ended, Nevills Rapids at the mouth of Seventy-Five Mile Creek shortly began, and they were an order of magnitude worse than the Escalante Creek rapids. An escape by river was impossible. I certainly couldn't swim up the river against that current.

So at 6:00 p.m. on Monday, I realized that the Grand Canyon had caught me in one of its oldest traps. It was like a fish trap, an easy door in with no way out.

I had obtained a hike permit from the Park Service and had indicated that I would be out of the Grand Canyon at about 6:00 p.m., Wednesday. That meant it would be forty-eight hours before I would be missed.

My prison was a jumble of rocks bordered in part with a lacey ribbon of sand. The delta at the mouth of Escalante Creek formed a rough triangle three hundred feet in height where it came out of the canyon wall and about six hundred feet across at the base along the river.

All I could do was wait either for the Park Service to become worried enough that they sent out a search party, which could be four or five days, or for a river party to float by, which might be tomorrow or in two weeks. A friend of mine had told me that there were float trips almost every two or three days. So this seemed to be my quickest means of escape. I fell asleep that night exhausted from my attempts to escape and full of worry and fear. About 2:30 a.m., I awoke and was pleased to see the stars brightly shinning above the black canyon walls. It was really dark in the canyon where no artificial light reached. I loved it. Before I fell back to sleep, a meteor flashed across the sky, disappearing to the south behind the black edge of the canyon wall. Listening to the gurgling noises of the river, I thought, *This is my universe, unbelievably beautiful and just as dangerous.*

Day Three

The next morning, Tuesday, I awoke with a clear mind and was able to better assess my situation. I had a full three days of food left, a signal mirror, a flashlight, and matches. I would conserve food and prepare as many distress signals as I could. I placed my yellow life jacket on a rock so it could be seen from the river, tied my white T-shirt to my walking stick, built three rock cairns so that they could be seen from the river, laid out my sleeping bag in a seven-by-seven-foot square and then placed my white map in a three-by-three-foot square on it, built three piles of firewood, and waited.

I had a whole river of water, and the delta was loaded with rattlesnakes, so I wouldn't starve. All I had to do was wait, and that was the hard part.

There were only a few places where you can enter the river with a boat and only a few places to camp. So most float trips start at the same place, camp at the same places, and travel the same parts of the river at similar rates. Therefore, I assumed that I could expect a boat at or near the same time I had encountered the boats on Monday morning.

About noon on Tuesday, I realized that indeed the river had been rising. Something was amiss here; I had checked before leaving and the Corps of Engineers were not planning to increase the output from Glen Canyon Dam. Where was all this water coming from? It was muddy and full of trees. Water from Lake Powel was clear and cold; this water was warm. Now it occurred to me, the thunderstorms of Sunday evening that I saw as I fell asleep didn't dump any water on me or the Grand Canyon, but they saturated the nearby watershed of the Little Colorado River. The Little Colorado River joins the big Colorado River just six miles upstream from the Tanner Canyon Rapids.

Torrential rains and catastrophic floods gave a good picture of the late summer thunderstorms that were generated on the Coconino Plateau. The hot high-desert rocks create giant convection cells during the day that sometimes punch towering cumulonimbus clouds through the tropopause. The sun sets, and the whole mess condenses into liquid water and collapses onto the desert floor. The channel of the Little Colorado River can be as dry as a bone one minute, and thirty minutes later, will be a raging flood of muddy water twenty feet deep. That was what I was watching when I fell asleep on Sunday night.

I don't think I slept on Tuesday night. I lay on my sleeping bag and watched the stars creep over the black edge of the canyon rim, march across my black-bordered patch of sky, and disappear behind the blackness on the other rim. Several glowing meteors sliced across the strip of bright, twinkling stars overhead. I lay there, listening to the sounds of the canyon. The gurgling and splashing of the river water had a slow rhythm to it that was most likely being influenced by the oscillations of the water chute just upstream. Every now and then, I would hear the fall of rocks down the nearby canyon walls. This was the unrelenting work of gravity and weathering on the rocks.

The nearest human was miles away on the high rim. It's a strange feeling one gets being this isolated and remote. It's not a bad feeling; it's just different, a feeling that there was just you and the universe. There was nothing else in the dark to reach out and touch but the rocks of Mother Earth.

Day Four

On Wednesday morning around ten o'clock, I sat anxiously on a rock, looking up the river for a boat. I was a little numb from not sleeping, and it took me a couple of seconds to identify the vibrations I was feeling in the rock. A jet airplane was coming up the canyon from the southwest. I looked around, and an F-4 Phantom shot through the slot of the lower canyon about six hundred feet above the river. The pilot was rolling the jet over on its side in order to make the turns in the canyon. I could see the pilot and every detail of the airplane. I watched in awe as he disappeared upstream. The sound had been overwhelming. Then I heard a second one coming. Damn, where was my signal mirror? The second phantom had followed the first out of sight by the time I found my signal mirror. That was incredible flying. If there were two, then there might be more. I sat with my signal mirror, alert and ready for the next aircraft. Ten minutes later, I heard another jet coming up the canyon. As he rocketed through the slot, I tried to flash him with my signal mirror. By the time he passed me, I could see the flash from the mirror on the jet. Now I was ready, and when the next one knifed into view, I had flashes of light playing all over his aircraft. He was coming right toward me when I played flashes of light over the cockpit. I felt sure he had seen me. Sure enough, five minutes later, here he came. He roared into view, pulled the nose of the airplane straight up, fired his afterburners, and did barrel rolls out of the canyon. I was blown flat by the shockwave from the afterburners. There was no doubt I had been seen, and rescue was imminent. Rocks fell down the canyon walls for ten minutes after this performance. Man oh man, I wished it had been me flying that phantom.

For the rest of the day, I watched in vain for a boat or more airplanes. It finally sunk in that the jet pilot wasn't going to report a stranded hiker in the canyon. He had noticed me and had decided to just show his stuff. I must admit, it was impressive, and the sort of thing I would never forget.

Wednesday night was spent much like the previous one. I would sleep for an hour or so, then wake up, and watch the stars and meteors. Throughout the night, rocks would fall down the canyon walls, some near and others far away. I wondered if the wild goats were causing some of these rock falls, then I realized the goats were probably much too smart to be walking high up on the canyon walls in the dark. I've never heard anyone else mention the rock falls. I've heard them on every overnight trip I had taken into the canyon.

Accounts of other peoples' trips into the canyon always seemed obsessed with food. They never take the time to just listen and feel the canyon. The little things like the microenvironment next to the river are ignored. If you are more than two hundred feet above the river, the air is very dry, and the only smells are of dirt and rocks. As you walk down toward the river in this last two hundred feet, you can feel and smell the humidity slowly increase. When you reach twenty feet above the water, you are overwhelmed with the smells of vegetation, mold, mud, and wet sand. As you dig around in the boulders next to the channel, you can smell the rat droppings and the snake dens. Seemly, out of thin air, ravens will show up when you are digging around in the boulders. Either they're hoping you'll flush out something to eat or you're the most entertaining thing they've seen in weeks. Ravens will eat carrion; perhaps, they're waiting for me to die. Then this group will be first in line for the best parts.

Day Five

On Thursday morning, I lay on my sleeping bag, watching the stars disappear into the steadily brightening sky. Slowly, the northwestern walls of the canyon became awash in sunlight as the shadow's edge from the south rim slid down toward me. The rats, insects, and birds were about their busy lives long before the sun itself peaked over the rim.

It was midmorning, and again, I sat on a rock with my T-shirt flag, looking up the river and checking my watch. I noted the time, 9:56 a.m. and looked up the river; there was a boat, no two boats. I jumped up and started waving my T-shirt flag.

The two boats came floating down the river until they were about three hundred yards from me when the lead boat turned toward shore, and a tall blond-bearded man stood up and waved me over to his boat.

"What's wrong?" he asked. "Who are you? How long have you been here?" I told him that I'd hiked down the Tanner Trail and was headed to the Hance Trail, but high water had stopped me from getting there. "Wow!" he exclaimed. "Are you hungry? Were you scared?"

I assured him I wasn't hungry; however, I had been somewhat worried about getting out of here. I asked if I could have a ride downstream to someplace where I could walk out.

"Sure," he replied. "Get aboard and we'll give you a ride all the way to Phantom Ranch. Tell us about your hike. What did you see?"

I was rescued; I was mighty happy. The people in the boats wanted to hear every detail of my trip. I had to tell about the ride through the whirlpool twice.

The boat ride itself was exciting. The expedition leaders were apprehensive about running the Nevills Rapids because of the high water; therefore, before we left my campsite, they made sure that everyone and everything were securely positioned in the rubber boats.

What a ride! The boats nearly stood on end, going through the Nevills Rapids. I was sure I would not have made those rapids alive on my air mattress.

About fifteen minutes later, we encountered the Hance Rapids. They were exciting; but compared to the Nevills Rapids, they were definitely no challenge.

A few minutes later, we floated across the great unconformity that exists between the Dox Sandstone and the much older Precambrian rocks of the Inner Gorge. More than a billion years of time was not represented here. Time in which there was not any form of life larger than a single cell on Earth, and a steadily decreasing rain of meteors pounded the atmosphere, oceans, and rocks.

The most amazing thing about the metamorphic rocks of the Inner Gorge is not their age, but their surface. The thousands of years of sand and silt carried by the Colorado River have polished them until they shone like tombstones. Boating down this canyon of polished rock gave me the feeling that I was floating through a giant cathedral.

Four hours after being rescued, I was at Phantom Ranch and was anxious to hike out on the Bright Angel Trail.

I left Phantom Ranch on the Bright Angel Trail at 3:15 p.m. and reached Indian Gardens at 7:00 p.m. I rested there for an hour then left for the rim with 4.5 miles of trail to walk and 3,500 feet to attain vertically. My rests were frequent and long. At four thirty Friday morning, I reached the Bright Angel Lodge. At 4:45 a.m., I reported to the district ranger's office that I was safely out of the canyon.

The ranger inquired, "Did you have a nice hike?"

"Unforgettable," I replied.

Grantsmanship

In the 1960s, a terrible thing happened to science. In order to fund science, scientists had to write proposals for money to finance politically correct projects. This was referred to as grantsmanship, and the money was referred to as soft money. This was a form of begging that pitted scientist against scientist. Begging for money to finance politically correct projects is what funds projects today and is the reason that science in government agencies is a complete farce. Any proposal that a scientist writes today will not be funded unless it appears to be politically correct and contains the right amount of buzz words like *hyper, multispectral,* or *catastrophic.*

Please understand that although I'm opposed to grantsmanship, I was very good at it. I used it to fund great projects while working for NASA and fantastic science projects over much of Alaska.

Near the end of the Apollo program, NASA sent out a request for proposals concerning a special test site on Earth to use to test the effectiveness of instruments in Earth orbit for geologic applications. I was one of nine scientists who presented proposals. Only my proposal was funded. Hey, I told you I was good at this. What really upset the other eight scientists was that I was the only one that did not have a PhD. They actually tried to have me disqualified over this. At the end of this project, I entered a PhD program in geology at the University of Arizona and quickly finished my degree in two and a half years. Now I had my union card, so to speak, and set out to learn the secrets of the universe.

Perhaps now you see the beginning of a rogue scientist. I wasn't a troublemaker; I loved science and worked hard to be the best at whatever I was doing. During the Apollo program, I was introduced to a well-known geologist at the US Geological Survey in Denver. He had spent the last twenty-five years mapping a single fifteen-minute quadrangle in the edge of the Rocky Mountains. He had also published a paper about this area every year. He even owned a house in the area.

I was stunned. I had mapped an area nines times the size of this area in one year, had published a paper on it, and had moved on to other mapping projects. This was truly what was labeled by many as elitist welfare. He did not have any intention of finishing the project; nor had he gotten any encouragement to do so.

The test site that I created for NASA was an area twenty miles square and centered about the small town of Mill Creek, Oklahoma. It contained everything that NASA had requested: nearly pure silica rocks, clean carbonates like limestone and dolomite, and classic igneous rocks such as granite and basalt. I was happy, NASA was happy, and the science of remote sensing was born. The first image processed in the Landsat series of Earth resources satellites was of the Mill Creek test site.

Over the span of three years, imagery and photographs of all types were acquired of the Mill Creek test site from orbiting vehicles and aircraft. I now had data of a known area that covered most of the electromagnetic spectrum.

While I was in graduate school at the University of Oklahoma, I took two semesters of a graduate course in quantum chemistry. At the beginning of the first semester, I was shocked. This was the real science; all those undergrad courses in classic physics and chemistry were garbage. Now I understood the interaction of matter and electromagnetic radiation. Now things made sense!

The Mill Creek test site had become my universe, and quantum electrodynamics was my game. Much of the data that I had acquired was classified, and I had to have a top secret security clearance to look at it. I was allowed to view some of the radar imagery only while in a vault in Houston. At the end of three years, I knew what most rocks looked like in any part of the spectrum. I had become one with quantum electrodynamics, referred to by most scientists as QED. I had become a remote-sensing specialist.

At this point in my life, someone offered me a job teaching and doing research at the University of Alaska in Fairbanks. I headed north, but I had learned too much. NASA kept a string on me, and I continued to do consulting work for them for the next ten years.

North to Alaska

I arrived in Fairbanks at the end of August 1974. Fall had already begun. The aspen and birch trees were cloaked in bright yellow leaves. Fall would be short, and the snow that fell at the end of September wouldn't melt until the next May.

Winter in Alaska has an austere beauty of its own. Living through a winter in Fairbanks takes a lot of determination. There is snow that doesn't melt, and in the middle of it, you get short days with only a few hours of twilight around noon each day. During my first January there, it dropped to minus 65°F and stayed there for two weeks. Even if you live in a modern house, it takes a lot of effort to survive.

In 1898, my mother's father walked over the Chilkoot Pass and stayed three years mining Klondike gold outside of Dawson. This had always given me a feeling of attachment to the far north.

I had definitely come to the right place. Fairbanks was a town where people parked their airplanes in their front yard, and I had a pilot's license. I had accrued more than 350 hours of pilot-in-command time, and there were plenty of planes for rent.

Teaching at the University of Alaska would turn out to be a better teaching experience than I had experienced elsewhere. You don't spend the winter in Fairbanks going to school unless you're seriously interested in your education. Most of the students were there to learn. I taught courses in geomorphology, aerial photograph interpretation, remote sensing, and research methods. The research methods course was a lot of grantsmanship, which is useful in most any professional job.

In later years, students would tell me that they greatly appreciated my teaching because my courses were the only courses that had helped them earn money. If there was a reward for teaching, this was it.

During the past twenty-five years, students and others would ask me what they could do to enhance their employability. My answer was quick: "Learn Chinese."

I had to pass reading proficiency exams in two languages for my PhD at the University of Arizona. I fulfilled that requirement with German and Russian. I went beyond what was required in Russian by learning to speak it well enough that I could communicate with a Russian and type it at thirty-five words a minute. Several times, I've gotten consulting jobs not because I was the best geologist, but because I was a geologist who could speak and read Russian. Knowing Russian made me a lot of money. You can measure the value of knowing a foreign language in dollars.

Grantsmanship immediately got me funding for projects through the University of Alaska across the entire state from Sitka to Barrow. Like knowing Russian, having a pilot's license in Alaska gave me opportunities that otherwise would not have been accessible.

My first project in Alaska was to gather baseline data along the north shore of the Gulf of Alaska for NOAA. I started my first day of fieldwork by landing on a small bush airstrip between the front of the Malaspina Glacier and the beach. I unloaded my pack containing the sampling gear, shouldered it, and headed for the beach. I was carrying my .357 magnum in a shoulder harness, not expecting to see any bears.

When I was within about thirty yards of the beach, the trees thinned, and I spotted a large grizzly on the edge of the back beach where the trees stopped. I stopped, but not soon enough. He lifted his head and started walking on all four paws toward me. I pulled out the gun and fired a shot into the air. Wow! I got one of the worst shocks of my life. He stood up on his hind feet. He must have been twelve feet tall.

I had five bullets left. I didn't feel there was enough firepower to stop a beast this big, so I took a chance and unloaded the gun at his feet. Rocks, sparks, and bullets were flying. He looked at his feet, turned, and ran off down the beach on all four feet.

That's when I got my second shock. He was unbelievably fast. There was no way a human could outrun a bear.

I squatted down by a tree and quickly reloaded the gun, all the while looking around for more bears. I slowly stood, looked around, took a few breaths, and started walking westward through the trees, paralleling the beach in a direction that was opposite to the direction in which the grizzly had run.

Now I was carrying the gun in my hand so it would be more readily available.

I had walked about one hundred yards through the trees when I spotted a sow with two cubs playing on the beach. They had not spotted me, so I walked a little farther back in the trees and then continued my westward walk.

I had walked nearly two hundred yards when I spotted another solo large grizzly. He was busy digging for something on the beach, so I started walking north to where I had left the airplane.

I hadn't been in the Alaskan bush for even thirty minutes, and I felt as if I had been dropped into a war zone. I had planned to camp out on the beach. Suddenly, it didn't seem like a good time to pitch a tent and build a fire on the beach. I got in the airplane and flew across the bay to the charming little fishing village of Yakutat.

At that time, Yakutat had a population of about 650 people and, like most Alaskan villages, at least three times as many dogs. On the edge of the ramp at the airport sat the very rustic Yakutat Lodge. I rented a room and a very rusty Ford Bronco. I got my gear from the airplane and started sampling areas that I could access with the Bronco.

That evening, during supper at the lodge, some of the local villagers filled me in on the bear problem. For some reason known only to the salmon, the salmon run was late, and the bears were wondering what was wrong and had left their favorite fishing holes up the streams and had wandered downstream to see what was holding up the salmon.

I had plenty of work to do that wasn't on the beach, so I worked on that until the salmon began to run about eight days later. People often asked, "Did you get any photographs of the bears?"

At the time, the thought of taking photographs didn't occur to me.

Malaspina Glacier

Later that summer, the forces of nature threw one of its famous Gulf of Alaska storms at Yakutat. I got in the leaky Bronco and drove around the Yakutat Forelands, observing how the energy of the storm was being expended on the beach, the rocks, and the trees. The wind was running to gusts of eighty miles an hour and was trying to convince the Cherokee Warrior (November-one-zero-six-Tango-Alpha) that I flew here to fly away from its tie-downs.

Even for a person who had been raised in Tornado Alley, this was impressive. The waves were awesome! Yakutat is world-renowned for its surf. The rainfall averages 204 inches per year, and the snowfall runs around 150 inches a year.

During the calm before the storm, I had noticed how flat and smooth the sandy beaches were. By contrast, the rocky beaches were steep. Two hours after the heavy rain, the storm was essentially over except for a strong wind out of the southwest. The ceilings were lifting fast, and I could see breaks in the cloud cover to the west. I decided I would fly November-one-zero-six-Tango-Alpha along the beach southward to Sitka and see if the storm had caused any major changes to the beach.

Flying the Warrior at three hundred feet above the beach, the rolling surf was a spectacular sight. Flying south of the Alsek River, the back beach quickly changed from trees to mountains and glaciers. A few of the glaciers extended from fourteen thousand feet to sea level. These are termed tidewater glaciers, and one of the most enchanting is La Perouse. It starts out as a narrow river of white ice that suddenly spreads out into a broad triangular shape that bulldozes the beach into an eighty-foot-high ridge of rocks and gravel.

Starting just south of the Alsek River, I encountered some light turbulence that was most likely caused by the suddenly rising terrain on my left and the choppy post-storm wind from my right. I was fascinated by the terminus of the La Perouse glacier because it was riven with crisscrossing fractures and ice caves.

As I approached the middle of the terminus, a gust of very cold wind sliding down the face of the glacier in the direction opposite to the offshore wind had rolled me inverted. My training kicked in, and I continued on through the roll until I was right-side up. This was unnerving because it happened so quickly, and I was only three hundred feet above the beach. I added more power and climbed to one thousand feet above the beach. I added cruise speed a little more than normal and flew over Cross Sound and headed to Sitka on the west coast of Baranof Island.

I filled the airplane up with avgas and took a break. Sitting on the stepladder which had been left next to the fuel pumps to help fuel high-wing airplanes, I contemplated the things I saw flying down the beach. The most significant was that at this time, right after the storm, even the sandy beaches were as steep as the rocky ones. This observation attested to how wave energy was spent at the beach interface. In the reports I prepared for NOAA, I used this observation and many others to address the effects of a major oil spill on specific areas of the beaches.

NOAA put my report in an open-file report so it would be readily available in case there was an oil spill. However, when the *Exxon Valdez* oil spill occurred, my report was ignored. As a result, the cleanup efforts directed by the government made the effects of the oil spill worse and longer lasting.

Natural oil seeps occur around a lot of Alaska, and perhaps the northeastern part of the Gulf of Alaska within two hundred miles of Yakutat has the most. On one clear sunny day, I flew N106TA to the Malaspina Glacier to hunt for rumored oil seeps. The seeps were difficult to spot because the vegetation grew over the top of them. The usual clue was a multicolored sheen of oil coursing down a stream; and occasionally, you would find an animal mired in one.

I quickly confirmed a natural seep on the eastern end of the beach in front of the Malaspina Glacier. It was trickling oil into Yakutat Bay and rapidly disappearing into the surf.

The seeps usually occur along large normal faults that dip toward the Gulf. This fault ran westward under the glacier, so I decided to fly along the beach in front of the glacier to where the fault reemerged near Kageet Point on Icy Bay. The storm had deposited a barge carrying railroad cars on the beach. Tank cars and boxcars littered the beach like toys. About three miles farther along the beach, a whale had been beached, and it was the center of attention. Birds, bears, and furry animals that I couldn't identify were tearing at its flesh and quarreling with one another. The whale lay near to where I had encountered the big grizzly on my first day in the field. I'm glad that I hadn't walked upon a scene like the beached whale. There's no telling what was hiding in the trees waiting for nightfall.

I couldn't spot the oil seep at Icy Bay from the air, and it was much too close to the party at the dead whale to land on the beach. I slowed the airplane, dropped a notch of flaps, circled two times, and took several photographs. There were no clouds over the Malaspina Glacier, so I headed east across it, back to Yakutat.

The Malaspina is so large it often creates its own weather. On a clear day like today, it's not usual to see a lone thunderstorm hitting the glacier with heavy rain and bolts of lightning. It is about 2,600 square miles, which is twice the size of the state of Rhode Island. Flying across it, you get the feeling that you're on another planet. Bands of highly fractured ice, loops of bare rocky moraines, and sinkholes in the dirty ice are all you see. If you crashed here and slid into one of the thousands of crevasses, no one would ever find you. It gives you a very creepy feeling.

Pictographs

The pictographs painted by ancient Indians in Horseshoe Canyon, Utah, gave me peculiar feelings of death and despair. They looked like human bodies that were shrouded in black and floating upright in the air. A few had eyes, others had headbands, but most were just solid black; and none had arms or legs. They were very haunting, but none fit my idea of an alien or shaman. They were unique, and I could not relate them to anything I'd seen before.

There was one question in my mind. *What had the Indians seen that they attempted to portray in the pictographs?*

A few years later, I was reminded of the pictographs while Russ (another geologist) and I were trying to retrieve some sand samples from a remote area south of Yakutat, Alaska.

Our objective was to collect several bags of sand from the south end of a barrier island by boat. It sounded like a simple task. You take a small four-man (at the most) boat down the Situk River to the north end of the barrier island and then motor down the long straight lagoon that's between the island and the mainland.

It was complicated with a tidal range of more than six feet and the entire area being rather flat. At low tide, the water was so shallow you couldn't motor the boat down or up the Situk River or along the lagoon. Therefore, we had to time our trip to the sampling area at one high tide and the return trip on the following high tide. Once you committed yourself to this trip, you were destined to enjoy to a twelve-hour journey.

Russ and I considered ourselves fortunate that high tide for the trip out was at 5:00 a.m., which meant that we would return near to 5:00 p.m. on the last high tide of the day.

It was very foggy as Russ and I slipped the boat into the Situk River. We couldn't see the far bank, so Russ carefully left our bank at a right angle, hoping that we would find the far bank before the combined current of the Situk River flowed and the ebbing tide carried us out to sea. The river was about two hundred feet wide at the boat landing, and Russ quickly put us in sight of the south bank. Moving westward with the outflowing current, the two miles to the mouth of the lagoon went by rapidly.

Russ headed us south down the center of the lagoon while I sat up front, looking through the fog for obstacles or things of interest. On the east shore of the lagoon, the ebbing tide was uncovering an extensive tidal flat.

The fog thickened to the point that our only guide was the water's edge. On our right, we couldn't even see features on the barrier island.

On our left, I couldn't see anything but fog. Then suddenly, in the mist where the tidal flat must be, I saw a dark figure that looked exactly like the black-shrouded figures I had seen on the walls of Horseshoe Canyon. I was getting a very creepy feeling, like I had just opened an ancient tomb.

"Russ, do you see that?" I asked in a loud whisper.

"What is that?" he responded as he slowed the boat to a crawl.

Two more of the figures loomed out of the mist, and I felt for my .357 magnum. Russ moved the boat until he grounded it on the shallow bottom next to the tidal flat.

There, standing upright on the tidal flat, were three eagles. They were patiently waiting for the ebbing tide to leave them something dead or dying on the muddy surface.

Was this what the pictographs represented? Eagles waiting in the mist!

Aniakchak Caldera

Yakutat is located on the northern part of the Alaska Panhandle, which is the extreme southeastern part of Alaska. Nine hundred miles due west across the Gulf of Alaska is the Alaska Peninsula. It is a string of land-tied volcanoes that continue southwest until they become the chain of Aleutian Islands. I had a new mapping project on the shores of Bristol Bay for NOAA. It included the beaches that ran from the Kvichak River north of King Salmon southward to Port Heiden.

The next spring, Larry sold the Cherokee Warrior and acquired a new Cessna 172 (N739PB). Niner-Papa-Bravo was a great plane for the work I was doing out of King Salmon. King Salmon is a key center for fishing in Southwestern Alaska. I was fascinated with the number and variety of aircraft that came and went out of the airport.

DC-3s, PBY Catalinas, C-130s, and Convair 990s were a few that came in and out within thirty minutes. DC-3s bring in fish from the small villages, and the other airplanes fly fish to the rest of the world.

The Alaskan peninsula is the eastern end of the Aleutian volcanic arc that has recently (geologically speaking) been uplifted. The chain of volcanoes sit on a wave-cut bench that has been gouged by glaciers and scoured by tsunamis. Oil seeps are numerous along the fault system that also facilitates the escape of volcanic materials.

Aniakchak caldera—perhaps the most spectacular volcanic feature in Alaska—is located here. It is the bowl-shaped remains of a volcano that blew off its upper part around four thousand years ago. It is six miles across and about two thousand feet deep. I had been working here for two weeks and had not seen the caldera because the whole area had been overcast, and the ceiling had not been high enough for me to see anything but the very base of the feature.

Today the clouds had lifted enough that I could see the tops of the jagged walls that enclose the caldera. I flew Niner-Papa-Bravo close to the walls on the west side and decided that there was plenty of room between the cloud base and the top of the jagged rock walls to let me fly safely into the caldera. I turned and flew into the caldera, dropping three hundred feet so I would stay clear of the ragged base of the clouds.

The immediate feeling was one of claustrophobia. I was flying a small airplane at 120 miles an hour in a giant room. My mind was doing flips over the sight picture. All I could see were walls of lava and cinders around me, a floor of small lakes and cinder cones below me, and solid clouds above me. I didn't see any signs of humans or animals or any sky or ocean; I could have been on another planet somewhere in the galaxy. What an awesome feeling; it ranks right up there with flying over the Malaspina Glacier.

I was so enthralled I didn't notice that the cloud base was lowering until I could only see the bottom of one notch in the walls. I dashed through it with fragments of clouds flashing around me.

In general, during the summer, bush pilots avoid clouds because the freezing level inside them may be as low as four thousand feet above sea level. Ice is deadly to small airplanes because it spoils the lift over the wings and adds weight. If I had crashed in the caldera, I doubt anyone would have heard the distress signal from my emergency location transponder.

Out of the caldera, my senses felt that things were now normal, and I got my mind back on track. Now I was looking for a small airstrip on the coastal plain that was used mainly by hunters. "More than long enough for a Cessna 172," one DC-3 pilot had said back at the old World War II army barracks that served as a hotel near the airport in King Salmon.

I found the airstrip about five miles west of Becharof Lake. The wind was at fifteen miles per hour out of the north. I made a left downwind so I could look over the condition of the airstrip and check for bears. Things looked good, so I made a steep approach on a short final with full flaps. I made a soft touchdown and flipped the switch to raise the flaps. Suddenly, I was decelerating, and I was not touching the brakes. My mind screamed soft runway; I ran the power backup and struggled to make a midfield turnout.

I shut the airplane down, set the brakes, and got out. Some gremlin in the back of my mind was asking, *Are we stuck here?* The material on the runway was a light fluffy mixture of silt and sand common to areas where wet ground went through a deep freeze-thaw cycle. No one else had been here since the last hard freeze. My tracks were the only ones down the airstrip.

While my mind tried to deal with this little problem, I walked over to the ten-by-ten-foot metal shack sitting on the edge of the turnout. The door and the corrugated tin walls of the shack were gouged with deep claw marks. The ground was littered with bear droppings. I recalled the encounter at the Malaspina Glacier and patted the .357 magnum hanging from my shoulder. The bear droppings looked old, and I didn't see any fresh tracks, so I walked out into the bush and grabbed a few samples.

A little later, I returned and loaded my samples and gear into the airplane. I walked to the middle of the airstrip and pondered my plight. The condition of the runway made my decision for me.

Under full power, I convinced Niner-Papa-Bravo to taxi to the north end of the airstrip. I turned around, and I could see my deep tracks stretching to the other end of the airstrip. I added flaps for takeoff, went to full power, and made my departure downwind on a soft surface.

I tell young pilots about this and ask them why I'm doing everything wrong. Few think it out. The runway dipped downhill to the south very steeply—at least ten degrees. I had to go downhill to get enough airspeed in order to get off the ground. On steeply dipping runways, downhill will often trump the wind direction. That's one of those things bush pilots learn that never affects anyone else.

A Floatplane Trip to Sithylemenkat Lake

I entered a left downwind on the east side of Sithylemenkat Lake in north central Alaska, forty miles south of the Arctic village Bettles. At the elevation of 1,500 feet above sea level, I slowed the Cessna 180 on floats to eighty miles an hour. Looking out the left window at the round lake, I checked for any obstacles or features that might prevent an approach from the north to a landing on the circular lake about three miles across, located at the bottom of a large granite bowl. The granite bowl is a crater created by a meteorite nearly forty thousand years ago.

Larry, my instructor, was sitting calmly in the right seat; and behind him sat my fifteen-year-old son, Kib. Kib was just along to test the fishing in the lake, and Larry was guiding me through my last lesson before my check ride for a seaplane rating tomorrow. This last lesson was about glassy water landings.

Landing a floatplane on water is usually a simple task. However, landing on clear water when there is no wind and no ripples on the surface to provide you with a reference for distance to the water's surface is a great challenge.

The approach is to set up a gradual descent that you carefully fly until you intersect the water's surface. Because of the drag created by the floats, floatplanes are easy to slow down. On the base leg of my approach, I turned on the carburetor heat, lowered the flaps two notches, and maintained enough power to keep a forward speed of about seventy-two miles per hour and a vertical descent rate of ten to twenty feet per minute.

I turned on a long final, and I was startled by what I saw. Before me, where the lake should be, was a hole in the earth to another sky.

49

The glassy surface of the lake was reflecting a part of the sky. There was no perception of depth, just sky above and sky where the lake had previously existed. I slowly flew into the hole with this creepy feeling that I was flying into another dimension. In my peripheral vision, I was barely aware of the shoreline and the walls of the crater.

Seconds after crossing where the shoreline must be, I was in the hole, flying with no physical references using only my instruments to keep my altitude. I checked my forward speed and my rate of descent. Everything looked good, and at that point, my son, Kib, started beating on the back of Larry's seat and yelling, "Dad, Dad, look. Look at the fish." I was too committed to my flying to look, and I yelled for him to shut up.

Seconds later, I heard the *tik-tik* of the floats hitting the water and felt the drag slow down the floatplane. Suddenly, my sight picture changed. I saw the shoreline, and my mind accepted that I was moving in the middle of a lake. I pulled the power to idle and raised the flaps, and seven-eight-three-zero-Kilo came to a slightly rocking stop in the middle of Sithylemenkat Lake.

Kib was incoherently jabbering about fish, and Larry came to his rescue. "We could see schools of pike, probably six feet long, in the clear water," he said.

I lowered the water rudders and slowly added power, and we started to plough across the lake like a boat. As I added more power, the floatplane rose up onto the steps and drag was reduced, and we began to ski on the water at sixty miles an hour. The step was the front half of the floats, which were about four inches deeper in the water than the back half. As you could imagine, water taxiing is boring; however, step taxiing is almost as cool as flying.

Floatplanes have no brakes; therefore, docking is done as carefully as it is in any boat. You have to cut power early and slowly coast into shore.

By the time I had the Cessna 180 tied to bushes along the shore, Larry and Kib were fishing. It was time for me to collect rocks for analysis. In the previous year, I had published a paper in the journal of the American Association for the Advancement of Science, reporting that Sithylemenkat Lake was located in a crater created by an ancient meteorite impact. Having mapped tens of thousands of impact craters while working in the Apollo Moon Program, the origin of the crater was obvious to me; however, the government geologists that worked here for three summers in a row were very upset that it had been, in fact, an obvious feature that they had missed.

Larry and Kib put over two hundred pounds of fish in the floats to fly back to Fairbanks.

By the time that I had finished my seaplane rating, I had accumulated more than five hundred hours of flying time, and a third of those where in Alaska. I was becoming a pilot with a lot of confidence in my abilities.

Flying the floatplane really opened up my access to a lot of Alaska. It allowed me to get a lot of work on the North Slope and along the coast of the Beaufort Sea (Arctic Ocean). I was hired by both the State of Alaska and NOAA to investigate the stability of the Alaska shoreline and to determine the origin of the islands that bordered this arctic shoreline.

Although the United States Geologic Survey had spent years here and had published maps of the area, I was sent out to redo it. Geologists and engineers working on activities relating to the development of Prudhoe Bay had discovered major problems with the published data. My observations of the current mapping projects of the USGS and other government agencies indicated that they showed up around June first and left about September twenty-fifth. Very little (if any) science was done, but a lot of fishing and drinking was performed.

If you are studying the processes related to stability and erosion in the Arctic, you need to be there before breakup and during freeze-up. They only stayed when the weather was nice and then returned to California and wrote fiction.

The Departure Stall

Home to seven-eight-three-zero-Kilo was the freshwater pond at Metro Field on the south side of Fairbanks. The summertime algae bloom in the pond was surprising to me because of its extent. In spite of the cold temperature of the clear water, the bright sunshine and long days produced a bumper crop of algae. Over time, the algae had produced a knife-sharp freshwater line along the length of the floats.

This is the sort of little thing that pilots notice because they are paying attention to minor details that might affect the performance of the airplane. This waterline was handy because it would indicate that I was overloaded at some remote lake if it was too far below the lake's surface. Conversely, landing on the cold (29°F) and salty water of the arctic bays and lagoons produce a reverse effect. Here the waterline would regularly ride three to four centimeters above the water's surface—a great lesson in the effects of density.

During the first summer after the completion of my seaplane rating, I had a few notable lessons. Perhaps the most important was the practice of a departure or power-on stall. Throughout the early part of my flying career, I would practice the recovery from stalls and instrument flying, just to keep my proficiency current.

On one of these occasions, I realized that I had not done a full-power departure stall in the floatplane. A departure stall occurs on takeoff when your engine quits or your airspeed gets too slow. This is what killed Wiley Post and Will Rogers twelve miles south of Barrow, Alaska, in 1935. They had fuelled up with dirty fuel in Kotzebue, Alaska, just before the visit to the hunting camp; and when they took off, the engine died from fuel deprivation. I had recovered many times from departure stalls in other aircraft quickly and easily.

I climbed seven-eight-three-zero-Kilo to 6,500 feet over the Tanana Flats and leveled out. I decided to first practice an approach stall. I turned on the carburetor heat and dropped the manifold pressure to fifteen inches. Slowly pulling aft on the yoke, I let the airspeed drop until I could feel the fluttering motions of a beginning stall. I pushed the yoke forward, turned off the carburetor heat, and pushed the throttle to full power. The Cessna quickly recovered, and I climbed back up to 6,500 feet. No surprises there as Cessnas are known for their great stall-recovery abilities.

In order to practice a departure stall, I pushed the throttle to full power and put three-zero-Kilo in a normal climb. I was duplicating the characteristics of a normal takeoff, or departure. After about twenty seconds, I pulled back on the yoke, slowly bleeding off the airspeed. I was expecting the normal shuttering of the plane as a stall developed across the wings. The wings are shaped so the stall does not occur over the entire wing at once.

This was what I expected; instead, I got one of the most frightening experiences of my life. As I reached about 65 mph, the airplane suddenly nosed over, and I began to dive vertically, nose down with full power. I was looking forward and straight down, and my airspeed was climbing fast. All I could see was the lush green swamps of the Tanana Flats.

I cut my power and pulled back on the yoke. Nothing happened! I was falling out of the sky, and my airspeed was rapidly increasing. I stood on the pedals and pulled with all my strength on the yoke. I was thinking, *Please don't let the cables snap.*

I rocked my wings back and forth. Slowly the nose began to rise, and the airspeed dropped. I added a little power, and then seven-eight-three-zero-Kilo picked up her nose. And quickly, everything was back to normal—except me! I was never the same again. I was at 2,500 feet; I had just fallen four thousand feet. On the original climb, I thought about starting this at 4,500 feet, but I decided to be overly cautious and climbed on up to 6,500 feet. The ground surface here was at nine hundred feet above mean sea level. I would have run out of air four hundred feet too soon.

When I finally got my nerve up and asked my instructor what had happened, he yelled for about thirty minutes before I began to understand what he was saying. Part of the yelling included a statement that indicated that there was good reason why we had not practiced departure stalls in the floatplane. Everyone except me knew that was what killed Post and Rogers. Then he hugged me and told me he was glad that I was still alive. That's Larry, one of the world's greatest instructors.

What actually happened was that the big floats caused a lot of drag. Therefore, when you stall, all that drag plus the full power flips the plane on its nose.

I could attest; that was exactly what happened.

Fort Yukon to Tanana

When I arrived in Alaska, I immediately began to learn the terrain and the geology using maps and satellite imagery. Two large areas—one south of Fort Yukon and the other south of Tanana—were mapped as sand dunes. I had studied sand dunes and sand seas around the world and had not seen anything that had the topographic texture and terrain like these areas.

Travelling around the area south of Fort Yukon in the floatplane, I was really surprised to discover that the entire area that had been mapped as sand dunes was actually nearly flat layers of gravel. A few samples revealed that they were, in fact, gold-bearing gravels—what some geologists would call placer gravels.

This really had me puzzled. How could someone make a mistake like this?

A few days later, we had one of those CAVU (clear air, visibility unlimited) days. The weather service would report the visibility as better than eighty miles. This was an easy call because they could see Mount McKinley, which was a little more than eighty miles away from their office windows.

It was so beautiful, I had to fly somewhere. Unfortunately, I could not find anyone who could go with me, so I had no one to share this day with.

The wind was out of the south-southwest at about fifteen miles per hour, so I took off from the Metro float pond, heading west over the Tanana River at four hundred feet above ground level. This put me under the traffic pattern at Fairbanks International Airport and south of the runways.

As I flew over the confluence of the clear Chena River and the milky Tanana River west of the airport, I activated my round-robin flight plan from Fairbanks to Boney River and returned. The air was cool and smooth. November-seven-eight-three-zero-Kilo quickly climbed to my cruising altitude of 6,500 feet, and I cranked in twenty degrees of crab to the left, which gave me a ground track of almost true west.

From more than a mile above the ground, my view was awesome. On my left stretched the Alaska Range from behind me, and around toward the southwest as far as I could see. It is a monstrous row of snow-covered peaks that run for more than 160 miles, with Mount McKinley being one of the closest.

At the lower limit of the snow, the lush green taiga forest begins. It is a mixture of birch, aspen, and black spruce, which covers northern and central Alaska, northern Canada, and most of Siberia. The taiga completely covers the broad central valley of Alaska that runs east to west from almost the Canadian border to the Bering Sea. This valley is bordered on the south with the Alaska Range and on the north with the rolling hills of the central Alaska platform.

The Alaska Range is still rising at about one-half of a centimeter a year. As a result, this tectonic activity keeps tilting the central valley toward the north and forces the Tanana River to maintain its active course along the north edge of the valley.

Today I'm taking in all this tectonic grandeur and thinking, *God, I love this planet. It's beautiful when the weather's nice.*

The interior Alaskan village of Tanana is just west of where the Tanana River joins the mighty Yukon River. I located a stream that appeared to be incised into the area mapped as sand dunes. This gave me a canyon with bare walls that would provide me with good access to whatever comprised the mysterious sand dunes.

I circled until I found a lake about one mile long that was only half of a mile from the canyon. Flying south into the wind, I made a smooth landing and taxied back to the north end, where I tied up to a birch tree. I felt sure that the wind would continue to blow out of the south for the rest of the day; therefore, when I was ready to leave, all I had to do was untie and take off to the south.

The lake was beautiful; birch and aspen trees lined the water's edge. There weren't any black spruce trees in sight, giving the taiga forest a light and open feeling. This was perfect—less chance of being surprised by a bear in the trees. Small red squirrels and numerous birds cried out in alarm as I hiked through their virgin forest.

The stream bank was nearly thirty feet high, and I mostly slid on my seat to the bottom. The brush along the stream was thicker in the downstream direction, so I started walking upstream toward the south. Within one hundred yards, I encountered a place where the little stream had undercut the bank. I looked around and listened carefully, checking for bears. I set down my pack and took my first close look at the materials in the bank. The entire exposed area was composed of nearly flat layers of gravel.

I removed the gold pan from my pack and filled it with three handfuls of gravel. After raking the bigger pebbles from the gravel, I filled the pan with water and swished the water around until I saw a trail of fine black sand. I raked out more of the course rocks and refilled the pan with clear water. Now I swished the water around in the pan until the fine ribbon of black sand began to move. As the black sand moved, it left a small line of very fine gold behind.

I slipped my gold pan back into my pack and hiked on upstream until I found a side stream that would allow me a way out of the little canyon. The side stream nearly took me back to the south end of the lake. I reached the edge of the lake and took time to look and listen for bears. Satisfied that there were no bears near me, I checked the area between yours truly and the floatplane. No bear, but next to the floatplane—three yards from the shore and standing in water up to his knees—was the largest bull moose I had ever seen.

Two thousand–plus pounds of meat with a gigantic rack was calmly eating aquatic plants next to the floatplane. I wondered if I could scare him away, but he might get mad and attack the aluminum floatplane. That pile of bone on his head could easily destroy the floatplane, and angry moose are noted for stomping people to death.

I backed up to a birch tree and sat on the mat of roots, moss, and grass at its base. One good thing about Alaska is that you don't have to worry about snakes. The isolation was beautiful; I heard a few far-off birds and the snorting of the bull moose as he cleared his nostrils of water. I was 150 miles west of Fairbanks and about ten miles south of Tanana. If something happened to the floatplane, I could walk north to the Yukon River and eventually get rescued.

After about fifteen minutes, the moose lifted his head, snorted loudly, and walked out of the water and into the trees. I was upwind to him; perhaps he finally smelled me and decided to find a lake untouched by humans. As I took off, I thought about how beautiful the lake was now. And in three months, the leaves would be gone, and the dark, cold seven months of winter would be starting.

Now I knew what comprised the areas that were mapped as sand dunes, but I had no clue as to why they had been wrongly mapped. Two years later, the director of the Alaskan Division of Geological and Geophysical Surveys would call me and ask if the two areas were really sand dunes. When I told him what I had found, he asked, "Were they mapped incorrectly on purpose, or was someone really that stupid?"

I replied that I had no idea why they were incorrectly mapped. It would be another five years before I learned the answer.

A Loose Cannon in the Arctic

A good thing about teaching and doing research at the University of Alaska was the availability of eager graduate students who didn't hesitate to climb into an airplane and follow me anywhere in the bush. I greatly appreciated the trust and dedication they gave to me and our projects.

One of the projects funded by NOAA was to determine the origin of the barrier islands along the north coast of Alaska, bordering the Beaufort Sea. I began the project by visiting the islands with a graduate student. Stu was an excellent student that had spent two years with the air force in Antarctica. He had good survival skills and knew how to prepare for our trips into the remote Alaskan bush.

In the summer, the lagoons behind the islands become a soup of small critters. The birds that fly north to nest here immediately flush their newly hatched chicks into this soup. The chicks sit in this soup for about eight weeks, eating, growing, and putting on lots of fat. When they leave at the end of summer, the chicks are so fat that they can barely get into the air. Apparently, the fat gets them to somewhere far enough south that they can finish growing over the winter. Then in the spring, they begin the cycle again.

Stu and I began what was to become an extensive study of the north slope of Alaska by pitching our tent in the middle of one of the barrier islands. The surface of the island was covered with well-established tundra exactly like the tundra on the coastal plain. The frozen gravels that composed the island were identical to the frozen gravels that lay under the tundra on the coastal plain.

Being there and seeing the materials in situ made it obvious that the islands were remnants of the coastal plain carved out by thermal erosion or the melting of the permanent ground ice. Barrier islands around the world are usually created by the deposition of gravels and sand transported to their location by long shore currents. Since the publications by geologists of the USGS indicated that the islands had been created by long shore transport and there was no mention of thermal erosion, it became evident that they had never visited the islands.

The biggest surprise was yet to come. Publications by a government geologist indicated that the north slope of Alaska had never been glaciated. As Stu and I hiked around the islands, we encountered large rectangular blocks of granite scattered everywhere. The blocks probably weighed two or more tons and usually had one flat side covered with chatter marks. Crescent-shaped chatter marks are generated when boulders are drug over hard bedrock surfaces by glacier ice.

Throughout the rest of the summer, scientists from around the world came to see the boulders. This was a significant discovery and would change many theories on Pleistocene glaciations. The government geologist who had published the erroneous information tried to make NOAA stop sending new scientists to areas that he had published on and tried to get me fired from the university.

The surprises didn't stop. As Stu and I lay in our sleeping bags on one of the islands during the not-so-dark nights, we were shaken by multiple earthquakes. The published information indicated that the North Slope was seismically quiet. No earthquakes had ever been detected there. Actually, no seismic station had ever been placed there. No effort had been made to collect data on earthquakes. In the absence of data, government scientists concocted many wild theories and, of course, published them.

Doing fieldwork in the Arctic is dangerous, even in the summer. We were successful due to Stu's superior logistic skills. You can't stop at a convenience store if you have forgotten something.

I worked a total of fifteen years on the North Slope, in parts of the Brooks Range and along the entire Arctic Ocean shoreline from Demarcation Bay on the Canadian border to Nome. Additionally, I spent four years working on parts of the Arctic Ocean shoreline bordering Siberia. For a few years, I think Stu and I were the leading experts in the geology of the Arctic coast of Alaska. I did work for the federal government, the State of Alaska, the native corporations, and several oil companies.

Before the discovery of Prudhoe Bay, the USGS published a professional paper claiming that there was no oil in the area. Later, before the development of Prudhoe Bay, the USGS made a press release that there was no gravel in the area for the oil companies to use for the required drilling pads. The press release quickly prompted a phone call to me from the State geologist. I rapidly calmed his fears with the news that there was plenty of gravel in the area that was not in environmentally sensitive areas like in the middle of an active stream. I knew this because I had actually mapped the area. I had discovered numerous abandoned stream channels on the coastal plain. These environmentally secure areas would provide the oil companies with all the gravel they would ever need.

This brought to light these questions. Why do federal agencies do everything they can to thwart the economic engine that makes their existence possible? Are they this stupid, or is it some socialistic conspiracy to kill all private enterprise?

Snow-Blind

On a clear sunny day in April, I was driving a pickup truck from the Naval Research Station north of Barrow to the Barrow airport. Everything—including the Arctic Ocean—was still covered with snow or ice. The road was solid ice, made from a winter of hard-packed snow. It came complete with ruts and large potholes. In another six weeks, it would be mud and puddles.

Randy, one of my graduate students, was bouncing along in the truck with me. He came to Alaska in the military and, like so many others, just stayed. If you're the outdoor type and you get rotated to Alaska, it's hard to leave.

Randy is a pilot, and owns a twin-engine Piper Apache, which he uses for acquiring scenic aerial photographs of Alaska. We were about halfway to the airport when my eyes started trying to close involuntary. Finally, they closed and wouldn't reopen, and I brought the truck to a stop.

"What's wrong?" asked Randy.

"I can't see," I replied.

"You are suffering photokeratitis," he responded.

I was feeling panicky. "What's that?" I yelled.

"You've gone snow-blind. Where are your sunglasses?"

"In the airplane."

"Let me drive," he offered.

I opened the door and slid out of the truck. Randy guided me around to the passengers' side, and I climbed in. He took me back to the research station and put me in my bunk. An hour later, he woke me up, handed me my sunglasses, and asked, "How are you seeing now?"

"Better," I replied.

"Good," he said. "You stay inside until suppertime, and I'll get the rest of the camera gear out of the airplane."

A good thing about working with graduate students is that they're usually smart. Sometimes they are geniuses.

One of my graduate students, Tom, started his own consulting business when he graduated.

A couple of years after graduation, he asked me to fly him to some remote areas on the north slope of Alaska. He needed aerial photographs of streams that had been subjected to outburst flooding caused by the collapse of ice dams during the last one thousand years. The area located between Point Barrow and Cape Lisburne is the remote northwest coast of Alaska. It was in this area that Will Rogers and Wiley Post died on August 15, 1935.

We intended to fly from Fairbanks to Deadhorse, which is at Prudhoe Bay, to Point Barrow. We planned to fuel up at each of these places and then fly a round-robin from Point Barrow to Cape Lisburne and back. This was to be a long trip, but we had twenty-four hours of daylight, and the weather looked great.

The weather was clear over central Alaska, and from the Brooks Range north, it was overcast with high clouds and ceilings at nine thousand feet. However, the weather in Alaska can be summed up with one word: *surprise!*

After completing the round-robin, we landed at Point Barrow, fueled up the Cessna 172, and topped ourselves off with coffee. The weather briefing indicated that our ceilings had dropped to six thousand feet. That was not a surprise or a concern. Our next stop was Deadhorse, and the highest thing en route would be a musk ox.

A little more than halfway to Deadhorse, the ceiling began to drop, and the visibility was less than two miles. Keeping clear of the clouds, I had slowly worked my way down to less than one thousand feet above the ground.

Tom radioed Deadhorse for their current weather and discovered that they were in a classic Arctic fogbank—zero visibility and zero ceilings. The good news was that Bettles was still clear.

Additionally, the weather at Point Barrow was expected to soon be like Deadhorse, but the tops of the clouds were at six thousand feet.

Sometimes things seem simple when really they aren't. I headed the Cessna south toward Bettles and started a climb to the top of the clouds. I had always enjoyed flying on instruments, and today's climb was smooth and uneventful. In a few minutes, we were on top in the bright sunshine with the puffy tops of the clouds below us. Sporadic peaks of the Brooks Range rose out of the clouds, looking like islands in a fluffy white sea.

Then I had a terrifying realization. I was going snow-blind.

"Tom, can you fly the airplane?" I squeaked.

"Doc, you're crazy. I can barely see to drive a car, and I feel dizzy just thinking about it," Tom replied.

"Tom, I'm going snow-blind, and I left my sunglasses in the truck when we loaded the airplane," I explained.

"Shit, Doc! Relax, I got this."

Tom unhooked his seat belt, turned around in his seat, and emptied the rest of his Coke cans out of their cardboard box and then went to work on the box with his knife. Before my eyes shut down, Tom fashioned me a pair of Eskimo sunglasses from the cardboard. The two horizontal slits worked perfectly.

After fueling the airplane in Bettles, we took a break at the lodge. I drank a cup of coffee, and Tom downed a Coke.

"Tom, tell me why you didn't learn to fly an airplane," I asked.

"Well, Doc," he replied with a cigarette hanging between his lips, "I know you're into dials, levers, and numbers." He blew out what looked like a jet's contrail of smoke and added, "I'm more into piña coladas and well-tanned women."

The Multiengine Rating

Larry Chenaille ran an air taxi service and a flight school on the east ramp at Fairbanks International Airport. Larry had checked me out in several different types of aircraft before he schooled me through my seaplane rating. He used twin-engine Piper Aztecs in his air taxi service. They were rugged, fast seven-seat aircraft that had good short-runway takeoff abilities.

Having conquered seaplanes, I felt that I should move up to higher performance aircraft. I asked Larry if he would help me get my multiengine rating in one of his three Aztecs. "Of course," he replied. "However, we will have to work you in between bush flights." I was very excited about this; all that horsepower was a big lure for me.

My first lesson in November-one-zero-two-Juliet-Kilo came at the end of a day during which Larry had been flying to small villages in the Alaskan bush. Larry told me to taxi out for departure, fly over to the small town of North Pole, and perform a touch and go. Since I had flown aircraft with engines similar to the Aztecs', and I had experience in aircraft with variable pitch props plus retractable gear, Larry was assuming that there wasn't a lot left to teach me.

Ten miles south of the village of North Pole, I radioed Unicom and told them I was headed in to do a touch and go. It was at this point that Larry decided to accelerate my training. As I was talking on the radio, Larry pulled the throttle back on the left engine. Not expecting the sudden asymmetric thrust or knowing what to do in the event of such a situation, I let the power from the right engine flip us inverted. We're barely one thousand feet above the ground and hanging upside down in our seat belts. Larry screamed, "Jan, let me have the plane!" I turned the plane over to him. Larry put power back into the left engine and rolled the plane on through the roll until we're right-side up. Well hell, that's what I was going to do; he should have let me handle it.

I received my training for my private pilots' license at an aerobatic school in Arizona where being inverted in an airplane was an everyday event. Now, thirty-five years later, Larry admits that was the only time in his life that he has been inverted in a twin-engine aircraft. When he tells this story, I just smile and agree. I've never had the nerve to tell him that was just the first of many times I was inverted in a twin-engine aircraft.

Larry's air taxi business was in heavy demand that summer and opportunities for renting the Aztec for multiengine training were scarce. It was almost fall when Larry gave the bad news: he was going to sell the Aztec I was training in so he could buy a new aircraft of another type and that further training in the newer aircraft would be more expensive.

I was shocked; I liked this Aztec and renting it was already a bit expensive to me. I didn't like the idea of renting an aircraft that was more expensive and unknown. So on impulse, I asked, "How much do you want for the Aztec?"

Larry patted his beer belly, rolled his eyes, and replied, "Thirty-five thousand, and I'll throw in a fresh annual.

"You have a deal," I replied, and we shook hands. Thus began an eleven-year love affair with November-one-zero-two-

Juliet-Kilo. In fact, the Aztec was oftened reffered to as the other woman by my wife.

This purchase wasn't going to give me the grief that my first purchase of an aircraft did ten years earlier because this time, I owned a house. I bought my first aircraft before we bought a house, and for some unfathomable reason, this put a strain on the marriage and my happiness until I bought a house.

Winter came quickly in the Arctic, and soon, Larry and I resumed my multiengine training in November-one-zero-two-Juliet-Kilo in temperatures below zero degrees Fahrenheit. We would start practice with stalls and steep turns about a point and then finish up flying with one engine out. We left the single-engine work until the last because in the extreme cold, the engine we had shut down might not restart. This was the case for about half of the lessons, and I became very adept at single-engine landings in the Aztec.

When it came time for my multiengine check ride, it was minus twenty degrees Fahrenheit and clear. While going through the check list at the end of the runway, I discovered that the trim tab control for the stabilator was frozen.

"What are you going to do?" asked the FAA examiner.

"I'm going to taxi back to the aircraft hangar and fix it," I replied.

"Good answer," he said. "If you had answered any differently, you would have had to wait sixty days before we would have tried this again. As it is, we'll try again tomorrow."

The next day, the weather was the same, minus twenty degrees Fahrenheit and sunny. The trim tab control worked, and I took off without any problems. I was on the downwind preparing to depart the pattern to the practice area when I noticed a huge fountain of fuel coming out of the fuel port of the outboard tank in the left wing. The fuel cap had blown off, and the low pressure on top of the wing was quickly sucking the tank dry.

The examiner had noticed this spectacular display of sudden fuel loss, and with a wryly grin, he asked, "What are you going to do?"

"Land and fix the problem," I responded.

"That's the correct answer. We'll try this again tomorrow."

The Aztec has four fuel tanks, two in each wing, holding a total of 144 gallons of fuel. The loss of thirty-six gallons still left me with enough fuel to do whatever we were going to do today, but the correct answer was, "land and fix the problem."

The day of my third try was five degrees colder, but everything went smoothly, and I passed the check ride with compliments from the examiner. After he signed my logbook, it was 1300 hours, and I had at least an hour of daylight left, so I decided to take my first solo flight in November-one-zero-two-Juliet-Kilo.

It was December, and the sun was low on the horizon, but I couldn't wait to fly the Aztec solo. In the cold dense air, November-one-zero-two-Juliet-Kilo rose quickly to three hundred feet, and that's when I lost power. The pressure on the rudder pedals told me the left engine was out. Following my training, I quickly switched the fuel flow to the left engine from the left outboard tank to the right inboard tank and held my breath. In about three seconds, full power returned, and I continued on my solo flight. It turned out to have been just a little ice in the fuel line. A close friend of mine, who was a hairy-legged F-4 fighter pilot in Vietnam, once told me that's why we train for this shit because sooner or later it's going to happen.

The Taxi from Hell

Singapore is truly a city of gardens and temples. We had spent three exciting days there before our last flight on the trip to Indonesia.

The sun was setting as we crossed the equator high over the blue Java Sea. By the time we landed in Jakarta, the sun had completely set, and darkness had fallen over the tropics with the suddenness of a heavy drape pulled across a window at midday. We were ushered through customs with such speed and detachment that the feeling we received was one of absolute unconcern. The air-conditioned environment of the airplane and the terminal had provided us with no clues as to what lay outside. However, the greasy little company man who met us was indeed a clue. This dark sweaty troll looked as if he had slept in his clothes for several nights. At his beckon, we walked out the doors of the airport and stepped into hell. The moist heat, the smell, the noise, the traffic, and the crush of people hit us like a solid blow.

The fat sweating company man indicated a taxi for us to use, and this too was another clue. The taxi was dented and, in general, beat up—but nonetheless, it had been freshly painted red. A dark red like half-dried blood. Anita and I slid into the rear seat, and the little rotund company man, with his dark pudgy hands, slammed our door shut and got in the front seat next to the driver.

There was the smell of mold and brimstone as the driver started the engine. The engine quickly sprang to life with a roar of power and precision that was incongruous with the taxi's battered exterior. The driver activated the electric door locks, and the dull thud of the bolts sliding home was like the muffled slam of a coffin lid.

It was then that I noticed the driver of this taxi from hell. He looked like one of the animated dead—a zombie, or someone near dead and mad. This demon driver was completely bald, and the thin dark skin was drawn so tight over his head that you could see the sutures in his skull. His eyes bulged half out of his head, and his hideous grin revealed large yellow teeth that seemed to emit a sickly glow in the thick tropical night.

The engine exploded with power, and we accelerated into the dense traffic with an amazing surge of speed. The insane driver quickly attained a terrifying speed of more than 140 kph, skillfully weaving his way between vehicles as he shifted with long thin fingers and an arm so thin that it looked like a skeleton's arm. The long yellow fingernails on each bony hand seemed to glow like the teeth of this driver as he stared through the gloom with an evil leering grin.

The road was packed with traffic, but this wild zombie of a driver drove deftly through narrow gaps, which seemed to open magically for him. It was as if the horn, which the driver continually used, heralded our coming; and the hordes of small cars, trucks, and Bajajes gave way.

The sweat-cloaked company man with his close-set eyes and piglike nose pointed at an intersection and said something in Indonesian. This driver from hell slowly moved his head in a negative manner and pointed with those long yellow fingernails straight ahead. With the horn blaring, we blasted through the intersection, and the dark driver with black splotches on his skin never lessened his mad grin.

The traffic got thicker, and we came to an abrupt stop in a jungle of buses, taxis, trucks, and people. People were walking between the vehicles, hawking wares. Dirty half-starved children were staring in the windows of the taxi at Anita like they had never seen a blonde before. The backs of the trucks were full of dirty thin men, and they too were staring.

The heat increased, and the foul smell of sewage crept into the taxi. In a strained voice, Anita said, "Jan, where have you brought me?"

It looked, felt, and smelled like hell!

"Welcome to Jakarta," I said.

The devil's taxi and the traffic moved in spurts through the heart and heat of Jakarta, where the half gloom turned into a dimness punctuated with islands of bright lights. The sounds of vehicles and humans never lessened until we turned into the driveway that ran up to the front of the Sari Pacific Hotel. The sudden relief from most of the noise was greatly welcomed.

The Sari Pacific Hotel was a nice surprise; it looked clean. We walked into the sumptuous lobby and were greeted with an air-conditioned atmosphere that smelled clean as well as being cool. Thus went our first hour in Jakarta.

The hotel was nice. On the first day there, I had to go into the office, so I left Anita to cope as best she could. On that first day, Anita walked thirty feet out the front door of the hotel, turned around, and went back in the hotel. The next day, she got a perfumed hanky, and together, we made it all the way around the block that the hotel sat on. Her adjustment to the culture shock was steady, and soon, she was taking taxis to anywhere in Jakarta.

It does seem strange, but we never saw that blood-red taxi from hell again.

A Visit to Anak Krakatoa

Transportation about the island of Java is extremely varied. Jakarta and Surabaya, the two largest cities on the island, have four-lane streets packed with large buses and trucks that are interspersed with taxis, vans, and luxury cars. This would seem as traffic enough, but the spaces between the big vehicles are filled with small cars, motorbikes, scooter-powered three-wheeled Bajajs, pedicarts, and bicycles. At each intersection, skinny boys skillfully thread their way between the vehicles, hawking newspapers, cigarettes, candy, bottled water, and even food.

The two large cities sprawl for miles. The sky is yellow with smog, and the smells of exhaust and open sewers are overwhelming. The high-rise buildings of the intercity change into multistoried apartments, then single-story houses. The single-story houses lie behind a maze of high walls; they represent what is the middle class in Indonesia. Right next to these walls, an extensive, incomprehensible sea of shacks begins abruptly. The shacks appear to be constructed from the refuse of long-lost civilizations. No two are alike, made of paper, plastic, sheet metal, rags, cardboard and bamboo.

The roads turn into two-lanes, then become the classic island roads of one-lane overhung with trees. There are no speed limits; the traffic drives as fast as conditions allow. The blacktop becomes dirt, and right next to the edge of the single lane are small shops the size of refrigerator crates. Most are selling fruit, but some are selling gasoline labeled benzene by the liter bottle. Mothers nursing babies sit beside the shops, minding naked children that are playing among loose chickens and dogs. The air smells of overripe fruit, tobacco, and chicken.

The road is still packed with traffic, but its composition has changed. Now it is crowded with Asian-built minivans, motorbikes, and oxcarts. The number one rule is: the oxcarts have the right of way; beyond that, it's everyone for himself. It's not unusual to see a family of four all on one motorbike, sputtering and smoking through the traffic as fast as the overloaded vehicle will go. Occasionally, a young couple will speedily buzz by dressed in matching batik. The woman will often be riding sidesaddle with one arm tightly wrapped about the driver. Usually, the motorbike has been intricately painted in the same pattern that the riders are wearing. Thus, you become aware of one underlying aspect of Java: in among the poverty, chaos, and dirt, there is a deep reverence for art.

As you get to the more remote parts of the island, bridges become rare, and at each stream, there is a flourishing commerce in ferry traffic. If you're in a minivan as we were, there is an extensive session of haggling before a fare for our vehicle on a small pontoon boat can be struck. The motorbikes have a ferry system more in line with their economy. As we were sedately floated across the stream on the pontoon boat, dugout canoes scooted past us. In the center of each dugout canoe, a motorbike rode tied in an upright position. To the front and rear of the royal motorbike, the riders sat in the bottom of the canoe. In the rear, one small Javanese would be effortlessly paddling the dugout with the intensity that belied that he was late for another fare.

On the first four-day weekend, we took a minibus to the small town of Carita. It's located on the western end of the island of Java at the gateway to the Java Sea called the Sunda Strait. Near the center of the bay that is on the southwestern side of the strait are some small islands, which are the remnants of the original volcano of Krakatoa that exploded in 1883, creating a large caldera. In the heart of the caldera is a smoking volcanic cone referred to as Anak Krakatoa, which means the son of Krakatoa.

Because of the traffic on the island roads, it always takes twice as long as you have been told to get somewhere. We arrived after sunset, and the restaurant was closed. So we dined on candy bars and peanuts. The air-conditioning of our room on the beach consisted of open windows with no screens. The insect control was gecko lizards and bats. The beach was just fifty feet from our door, and the crashing of the waves completely surrounded us; therefore, I slept poorly.

The next morning was beautiful, and the beach looked like paradise. We ate breakfast and headed out to explore the beach. The beach has a steep face that drops vertically for twelve or fifteen feet; therefore, you can walk quickly from the dense jungle to the water's edge. By the time you're on the water's edge, you can no longer see your cabin or any other buildings.

This morning, we could see three small wooden boats about thirty feet long, serenely sailing about five hundred yards offshore. It seemed absolutely idyllic as we waded in the surf. Suddenly, out of the jungle, there appeared a young native man who introduced himself as Jasmine. He asked if he could get us some breakfast or drinks to which we replied that we had had breakfast and were now planning to do some sightseeing. This seemed to be a key term for him as he lit up with ideas for sightseeing. When he offered to take us out to the coral reefs on one of the small wooden boats, we immediately seized on the idea.

Jasmine disappeared into the jungle, only to return in about twenty minutes to where we were on the beach in one of the bright-blue wooden boats. He and two boys, his younger brothers, loaded us aboard; and thus we embarked on a fabulous adventure.

The wood in the boat had all been cut, shaped, and drilled by hand. It was held together with wooden pegs—no nails or screws. It had a small mast, but the sail was furled, and our power for this trip was to be a small outboard motor.

The crew of the boat consisted of the father (who owned the boat), his three sons, and his grandson. The oldest son, Jasmine, rigged up an oilcloth shade over part of the deck using poles and ropes tied to the mast. He was the only one of the group who could speak English.

As we started away from the shore, the small outboard motor died. It looked at least thirty years old. Jasmine assured us that this was not a problem as they had a spare motor that they could quickly run and retrieve. In fact, it was the number one engine that had just been repaired. We were greatly in luck.

The boys took the small motor off the boat and tied it to a pole like a freshly shot tiger, put it on their shoulders, and ran off through the surf and into the jungle toward home. In less than ten minutes, they returned with the number one motor swinging from the pole on their shoulders. Indeed, such a means of island transport is quick and efficient.

The number one motor proved to be much better than number two, and shortly, we were motoring out into the Straits of Sunda. For little more than an hour, we cruised over incredibly beautiful blue water under clear skies. From the railing, we could see the reefs and fishes as we slid through the amazingly calm water.

At some special point as determined by Jasmine, we stopped, and he helped Anita and me don our snorkels. Using a small ladder and a rope, he managed to get us over the side and into the clear warm water. It was a strange feeling when I let go of the boat and found myself floating freely in the water some three or four miles from shore. Something akin, I would think, to an EVA from a space station in orbit about the Earth. Guiding us slowly along, Jasmine took us on a snorkeling tour around the reef.

The reef was a stunningly beautiful environment. The corals were bright blues, reds, and pinks. The swarms of fish were all colors and sizes. This was Anita's ideal environment; she could float at the surface and just point, sending Jasmine and me diving to the bottom for choice pieces of coral. This undersea world was so entrancing that the time passed all too quickly.

As we leisurely motored back, Jasmine prepared fresh coconuts for us. It was a thrill watching him deftly peel, cut, and open the coconuts with a razor-sharp machete. We drank the cool sweet milk and scooped out the soft, sticky gelatinous meat. It was, of course, the best coconut that we ever ate on Java.

That evening, Jasmine's family cooked freshly caught fish for our supper. It was seasoned with local herbs and served on green banana leaves. Anita and I quickly devoured our fish and wished that we could have had more. Anita remarks to this day about how delicious that fish tasted.

Since the beach was so close to our cabin, we spent another night in the full surround sound of the surf. The next day dawned, and it was apparently going to be another beautiful day in this tropical paradise. It was a short ten-minute ride down a classic island road from the hotel to the boat harbor. The road was lined with palm trees, banana trees, and jungle plants in general. This morning, the road offered only a little traffic, mostly children and chickens with a few bicycles and pushcarts.

At the harbor, we boarded a new fiberglass motor launch that would take us out to the volcano, Krakatoa, in the middle of the Straits of

Sunda. There were sixteen passengers bound for the site of the most cataclysmic natural event in recorded history. It was in 1883 that the eruption of Krakatoa destroyed the huge volcano and sent shock waves around the world. Now, 106 years later, two Americans (Anita and I), two Welshmen, four Germans, three Brits, one Canadian, three Italian men, and one French bombshell in pink short shorts and high heels set off to view the holy spot. The French bombshell conned one of the Italians into carrying her video camera for her. It seemed that she was some type of journalist and needed to be in the picture, narrating what was being recorded as she stumbled over the cinders and chunks of lava. I think everyone on board had a tan of some sort except Anita, who was white with pink spots. She had gotten a lot of sun yesterday out on the coral reef. The crew of this boat was four young Indonesian men who spoke no English, German, or Italian but had decided to make a real effort to learn French.

On this beautiful morning, the sea was blue and calm. As we left the harbor, a school of dolphins gave us a short escort. I considered this a good omen. That and the fact that this boat's motor sounded in good shape made it a perfect morning. Later, I found out that the dolphins left us because we hadn't offered them any goodies for their escort service. Next time, I would come prepared.

It took two hours to reach Krakatoa. The trip would have been uneventful except halfway across the straits, the heat and motion of the boat caused my bottle of Bintang to explode. Bintang (which means "red star") is the major Indonesian beer. It tastes terrible but, not surprisingly, is the only beer available in Carita. The explosion filled the boat with the heady smell of warm beer. The smell of the beer made the Italians more frantic in their efforts to assist the French journalist with her video camera.

Only three island-sized remnants are left of the original volcano, Krakatoa. The three islands encircle a lagoon where the center of the volcano once lay. Now, this center is occupied with a new volcanic cone that has built up in the last twenty years. It is named Anak Krakatoa, or "The Son of Krakatoa."

The beach was made of black sand, and the water was so clear, you could see a coin on the black-sand seafloor in twenty feet of water. The smoking new volcanic cone rose nearly one thousand feet above this beautiful black beach.

This unlikely international group disembarked and took off to climb the black hill of ash and cinders. Their objective was to get a good view of the central vent from which steam could be seen slowly rising into the clear sky. The black ground was hot from the sun as well as from the geothermal heat. The beautiful clear sky let the sun shine on us with brutal intensity.

Most of us climbed slowly up the volcano in the heat while the Italians ran about like mad dogs. The French journalist climbed with Anita and me in her high heels, taking shots with her video camera and chain-smoking cigarettes. Everyone else had on tennis shoes.

During the time it took for the main part of our group to reach the summit pit, the Italians had run down the far side to the vent and back up to the rim where we were standing. This was done, I'm sure, to impress the French journalist. They stood around her gasping for breath with their tongues hanging out, boasting of their abilities.

The hot, steaming sulfur-lined pit looked like a lot of other volcanic vents I had seen around the world. Volcanic pits such as this lose a lot of their romance because they all smell overwhelmingly of rotten eggs. The Germans and I agreed that it looked like a doorway to hell. The French journalist panned the entire scene, putting us on tape for posterity.

We may have looked like we were close to death in that heat, and the Italians would have collapsed on the ground, but the ground was so hot that it was beginning to burn through our shoes. The most amazing thing was the French journalist, who continued to look cool and composed in her high-heeled shoes.

As we returned to the beach, everyone just kept walking until they were in the water. After an hour and a half on a hot volcano, the water was a welcome delight. We all, but one, went into the water over our heads to wash the ash and cinders off us as well as to cool down. The exception was the French journalist, who only waded in to the top of her pink shorts. She probably had to pee, and this was the only discreet way to do it on this trip.

The boat trip back was hot in the midday sun, but we were entertained by schools of flying fish, the amazing wave runners, and a large sea turtle who had, apparently, decided we were another turtle. I think we broke his heart as we left him in our wake.

The members of this diverse expedition had now become brothers-in-arms. They began to trade stories and become better acquainted.

The bold Italians spent the entire return trip collapsed on the deck. The last thing that I saw the French journalist videotaping was the Italians helping each other out of the boat. It was a hot and dirty trip, but I was very pleased that I got to visit the remnants of Krakatoa.

The next morning, Anita and I hired Jasmine and some of his friends to guide us to a rumored large waterfall high on the side of a volcano in the rain forest just east of Carita. It was a three-mile hike, but the morning was pleasant, and Anita and I thought we were still young.

As we walked along the path through the rain forest, we were treated with the sight of huge butterflies and an immense variety of tropical plants. Anita busily called out the names of plants that were used as houseplants back home. However, some of the plants were larger than a house. The rain forest was beautiful, but the vegetation was so thick that, at times, it was too dark to take photographs.

The narrow path took us nearly four thousand feet above sea level and more than three miles east of our beach hotel in Carita. Long before we saw the waterfall, we could hear it roaring through the forest. The rain forest is always noisy from the sounds of the insects and birds, but the thundering roar of the falling water drowned them out.

The narrow path broke out into a small clearing just above the waterfall. There, on huge rocks in the rushing water at the top of the falls, were about ten young Indonesian boys and girls picnicking, swimming, and diving into the plunge pool at the base of the waterfall. The waterfall was at least fifty feet high. The dives that the young Indonesians were making into the plunge pool were very impressive. They were greatly disappointed that they couldn't persuade Anita or me to make the jump. I would have tried the jump, but after the long hike (and we still had to hike back), I wasn't sure that I could have made the climb back to the top of the falls. We swam in the cool pools under smaller falls at the top of the big falls. We were nicely refreshed by the first really cool water that we had encountered since arriving in Indonesia.

Anita didn't want to leave; she had found her island paradise right here. Although she was the first to climb in the boat to leave Krakatoa, she was the last to leave the waterfall. However, she eventually followed us back into the rain forest—but with great protest. The trip back was as beautiful as the trip in, but I was disappointed that we didn't see any tigers or black rhinos.

As Anita frolicked in the cool pools of water at the top of the falls, ten young men in clean Levi's and khaki shirts came suddenly and silently out of the jungle and strode up to Jasmine and me. All were carrying machetes, and half of them were carrying automatic rifles. An intense discussion ensued between Jasmine and, I guess, the leader of the band of young men. It was all in Indonesian, and I could only guess by the urgency of the discussion that things were not good. Eventually, Jasmine turned to me and asked how much money I had with me. I opened my wallet and showed him that I had about four thousand rupiahs (about forty US dollars). He said he was very sorry, but these guys were rebels and didn't like foreigners. He had convinced them that we were unlike other foreigners; we were nice people and supported their movement.

I handed him all the money in the wallet. He gave me back about twenty rupiahs and gave the rest to the supposed leader. The leader thanked Jasmine and me—that much Indonesian I could understand. Then, by the time I had returned my wallet to my rear pants pocket, the group had silently disappeared back into the jungle.

We had an exciting trip to Krakatoa and an unforgettable weekend on the west end of the island of Java.

A Small Nick in the Prop

Seven miles south of the airport at Yakutat, Alaska, I was at three thousand feet above sea level and speeding along at three miles a minute. I radioed Yakutat Unicom that I was Aztec November-one-zero-two-Juliet-Kilo and requested traffic, wind, and active runway. Unicom replied that there was negative traffic, wind was one seven zero at one two, and the active was one-one.

I pulled the throttles back on the twin Lycomings until they both were at manifold pressures of fifteen inches. This didn't slow the aerodynamic Aztec down very much, but I turned on the carburetor heat to both engines, and the airspeed began to drop. I entered a right downwind to runway one-one, turned on the electric fuel pumps, and lowered the flaps one notch. This slowed me to 125 miles per hour, which was slow enough that I could lower the landing gear and the rest of the flaps.

As I lowered the gear handle, I saw, off to my right, the two huge six-inch cannons that sit on Cannon Beach. I got three in the green for the gear as I banked and turned right on a final approach for runway one-one. I visibly checked the nose gear in the small mirror to my left on the right side of the left engine. The nose gear appeared down and locked.

I trimmed the nose down a bit and pulled the throttles back a little. As I crossed the numbers on the end of the runway, I began my flare. I had been flying for nearly nine hours, and I was tired and stiff. However, I flared too soon, and November-one-zero-two-Juliet-Kilo quit flying about two feet above the runway. The main gear hit the runway with a bang. Two-Juliet-Kilo made a small bounce and then settled down, and I swiftly taxied to the fuel pumps.

It had been a long day. My younger brother and I had just completed a trip of nearly 1,500 miles from Corvallis, Oregon, to Yakutat, Alaska. It was beautiful clear weather the entire trip. We had fantastic views of Seattle, Washington, and Vancouver, British Columbia. The geologic panorama in just one day of rivers, volcanoes, islands, fjords, beaches, and glaciers was magnificent.

Yakutat is an old Tlingit Indian village with fishing still the main industry. The airport was built in 1939 as a secret Army Air Force airbase. We fueled up and tied down on the huge concrete ramp where B-17s and B-24s once refueled on their way to Ladd Army Airbase in Fairbanks, Alaska.

The Yakutat Lodge sits on the very edge of the giant ramp. The lodge contains a bar and a restaurant, which have large windows that look out over the ramp and runways. Both the bar and the restaurant are decorated with stuffed animals, giant fish, and other taxidermy nightmares. The walls and ceilings are covered with signed one-dollar bills. There must be one thousand bills or more. Some have been there for a long time; my name was on a few of them. A poem that I wrote about Yakutat hung on a wall in the bar.

As Tim and I sat looking out the windows during our supper of halibut steaks, admiring the collection of aircraft on the ramp, a DC-3 came chugging into view and stopped just outside the door to the bar. Such vintage aircraft still earn a living each day in Alaska. This old bird in its peeling red and white paint hauls fish every day from small villages to Yakutat, where they are then loaded on processing ships or flown on to Seattle or Anchorage.

The DC-3 pilot climbed out and made a brisk walk into the bar. Now this guy was the epitome of Alaskan bush pilots; he was wearing a plaid flannel shirt and sported a thick black beard. He sat down at a table and yelled for a beer and a steak in that order. The barmaid/waitress yelled back that the steak was on the grill and brought him a beer. He downed about one-half of the beer, belched, and looked around the bar and restaurant. He downed the rest of the beer and yelled, "Who's flying that little sissy twin out there on the ramp?"

"That'll be us," I replied. Tim had ducked and was trying to crawl under the table. I then volunteered that we were gold miners, and we just used the Aztec to fly back and forth from the mine to Fairbanks.

"Well, it ought to be good for that," he said. He took a drink of the second beer and offered to buy us a beer. Tim crawled out from under our table, and we joined Tom at his.

Two beers later, some of the locals showed up, and the card game began. At this point, it was after 2200 hours, and I was falling facedown on the table. Tim pulled me up by my collar and said, "Sorry, men. I've got to put my pilot to bed."

The next morning, at about 0800 hours, Tim and I entered the lodge for breakfast. Still playing cards and drinking beer, Tom and two locals told us "good morning," and I croaked something about an urgent need for coffee.

Fifteen minutes later, as Tim and I were eating breakfast, the guys folded the card game, and Tom announced that he had to go fly some fish. Tom finished his beer and walked a little unsteadily out to the old DC-3 and climbed in.

"What do you think he's going to do?" asked Tim.

"I think he's going to take a nap in the airplane," I replied.

There's a lapse of a few minutes, then Tom stuck his head out of the open window on the left side and screamed, "Clear prop!"

The radial engine on the left wing coughed and roared to life. As this engine revved up and started to run more smoothly, the right engine backfired, belched black smoke, and began revving up. Tom revved up the left engine even more and used the asymmetrical force to blast the tail around until he was pointed at the taxiway. He started to taxi then shoved the throttles to the wall and took off on the ramp. He climbed to about two hundred feet and turned south. He was going (presumably) to pick up fish.

Meekly, Tim and I carefully preflighted our sissy twin and then took off on runway two-zero and headed north to Fairbanks.

My weather briefing at Yakutat was mixed. It was clear from Yakutat to the Copper River and clear in Fairbanks. The satellite imagery indicated that there were clouds in the Copper River Basin, and because no pilots had flown through there this morning, there was no information on the base of the clouds. However, the tops had been reported at nine thousand.

The scenery on this flight was beyond anything that I've seen elsewhere. Streaking across the southern part of the Malaspina Glacier at the rate of one mile every twenty seconds at three thousand feet ASL, Tim remarked, "This is better than going to another planet."

I concurred, but it got even better. We had an eye-to-eye view of bighorn sheep on the mountains between the Malaspina Glacier and the Bering Glacier.

From a small airplane at three thousand feet, the Bering Glacier was a magnificent sight. It is a huge river of ice that flows down from eleven thousand feet to sea level. Where it terminates at the beach is a favorite haul-out area for seals. Hundreds of seals are frolicking on the beach and in the surf. Just west of the seals is a beachcombers' paradise where the flotsam and jetsam of the Gulf of Alaska collects. Abandoned ships and major pieces of airplanes litter the back beach.

As we flew across the wide muddy delta of the Copper River, we saw a tall wall of clouds filling the canyon. I dropped down to five hundred feet and attempted to look upstream, but the clouds went to the ground.

I added power to 75 percent and started a slow-spiraling ascent to the top of the clouds. As I gained altitude, the temperature dropped below freezing, and both engines began to run rough. I was getting carburetor ice, the bane of piston engines in Alaska. I turned on the carburetor heat and shoved the throttles to the wall. Two-Juliet-Kilo woke up like an angry dragon and began clawing at the sky.

At 9,500 feet, I could see across the tops of the nearest clouds. But to be safe, I climbed to 10,500 feet, leveled out, and headed north toward Big Delta. I turned off the carburetor heat and set up a cruise at 85 percent power. We reached the northern limits of the clouds just south of the Alaska Range in ninety minutes.

I spotted the Black Rapids ice field just south of Fort Greely and made a detour to show Tim the giant blue lake in the center of the ice field. In the early 1970s, when I first began flying in Alaska, I discovered the lake. I was extremely curious about what seemed to be an impossible natural feature. My first thought was that it was a volcano. But if it was a volcano, there would not have been an ice field. Ice fields have to collect snow all year to feed the glacier, and if a geothermal heat source was there before the ice field, then the ice field would have never formed. None of the other ice fields in Alaska had giant lakes in them. I checked this out by flying over several of them and looking at the others on satellite imagery.

Once on my many trips through Yakutat, I encountered an employee of the US Army Corps of Engineers who told me the origin of the lake. In 1962, Fort Greely received a nuclear reactor as part of a Cold War program to furnish military bases with nuclear power. According to my informant, they had a major problem in the mid-1960s that prompted them to pull the core and transport it to the middle of the Black Rapids ice field. In researching this possible cause, I did discover that of the nearly twenty reactors like this, the Fort Greely power plant was the only one that had no record as to what happened to its nuclear materials.

At the Black Rapids ice field, we dropped to 6,500 feet and flew westward on the north side of the Alaska Range. Within thirty minutes, we were circling the plateau that comprised the drainage divided between St. George Creek and Gold King Creek. My son, Kib, and his crew were building an airstrip of gravel on top of the plateau that was more than a mile long. It appeared to have be completed, so I landed. The landing was smooth and soft but very noisy as we kicked up a lot of loose gravel. My mistake. They had not finished packing the gravel, and my landing was a bit premature.

The post-landing inspection of November-one-zero-two-Juliet-Kilo revealed that the only damage was a small nick in the prop. It was about three centimeters in from the tip of one of the blades on the right prop and only a millimeter deep. I've had a lot worse on the floatplane.

Taking off in November-one-zero-two-Juliet-Kilo from Kib's airstrip on the plateau was one of the most enjoyable things I've done in an aircraft. With the wings clean (with flaps up), I would start rolling on the soft airstrip as I slowly throttled up to maximum power. When I reached the ground speed of sixty miles per hour, I would add two notches of flaps, and the Aztec would leap into the air. Slightly banking, I would turn right and dive into the one-thousand-foot-deep valley of St. George Creek. Shoving the nose down and bringing the landing gear up, I would raise the flaps, and the airplane would fall at a speed just above a stall for a few seconds until the forward airspeed made November-one-zero-two-Juliet-Kilo feel like a bird again. I would continue the dive until I was about fifty feet off the floor of the valley, at which point I would level out and go roaring down St. George Creek over the heads of the gold miners at 225 miles an hour.

At the mouth of the creek, I would pull back on the yoke until I was in a nearly vertical climb. When the stall warning came on, I would shove hard on the left rudder pedal, sort of fall over to the left, and dive back into the valley for another run. If someone finds flying boring, then they're not doing it right.

After I put the small nick in the right prop, I left Tim at the gold mine and flew to Fairbanks to find a mechanic. I found a mechanic who rounded out the nick with a file and told me that I would most likely have to replace the prop when the Aztec got its annual inspection next winter. That sounded good to me, and I started flying cargo and people back and forth between Fairbanks and the gold mine.

Gold mines in Alaska are small, nearly self-sufficient villages, and they attract a strange assortment of people. Thirty days after putting the nick in the prop, it became my duty to fly the camp cook and six hundred pounds of food from Fairbanks to the gold mine. The camp cook was a brassy blonde from New Jersey who talked often and loudly. Also, she did not like flying in small airplanes. Since she reminded me of Major Houlihan in the TV series *MASH*, I nicknamed her Hotlips.

It was one of those incredibly beautiful summer days in interior Alaska with not a cloud in the sky. We streaked across the Tanana Flats at three thousand feet above sea level, which was about the elevation of the airstrip on the plateau. This made things somewhat simple since I didn't have to descend to land on the airstrip. All I had to do was slow down, drop the flaps, lower the landing gear, and land. Hotlips had talked continuously since she had gotten in the airplane. Six miles from the airstrip, I started easing back on the throttles. The engine noise dropped to a point where I could hear Hotlips better than I wanted.

At that point in time and space, there was a god-awful *kawump* that shook the Aztec like we had been hit with flak. As I recovered from the flak hit, I became aware that Hotlips was screaming that she was going to die and that the right engine was vibrating somewhat stronger than it had before. Somewhere in the dim parts of my brain, there came a connection between the behavior of the right engine and the small nick in its prop.

I throttled back the right engine, and the vibrations became stronger, which made Hotlips scream louder. I throttled back up the right engine, dropped the landing gear, and made a very quick landing on the airstrip.

I killed the engines and shoved a screaming, cursing Hotlips out the door. Ya gotta wonder where a woman learns language like that.

There was a hole the size of my fist in the right side of the Aztec's nose that ran all the way to the left side. There, lodged in the skin on the left side, was the tip of the prop. I still have that prop tip.

I took off with the right engine shaking my teeth; but once I was airborne, I feathered the prop and killed the engine. I didn't want the right engine to fall off when I was somewhere in the middle of the Tanana Flats. The Aztec could fly on one engine for a long ways, and landing with one engine was easy.

When I got within twelve miles of Fairbanks, I radioed approach control and told them that I had lost an engine and requested a straight-in approach to the longest runway. They immediately cleared me for a straight-in approach to runway two-left.

Flying a twin with one engine out takes a lot of attention; you fly with the wing of the bad engine up higher than the other wing. This is called flying into the good engine. This, with a lot of rudder control, can keep the airplane in almost a straight line.

As I began my descent to two-left, I noticed the fire trucks. They were lining both sides of the runway for nearly a mile. At this point, I realized that someone thought that I was going to crash. Perhaps they were hoping that I would crash so they could try out their new fire-suppression equipment. Were they going to charge me for this?

I made a perfect engine-out landing. The control tower congratulated me, and the fire trucks drove away somewhat disappointed.

Negative, Three in the Green

"Shawnee Unicom, Aztec November-one-zero-two-Juliet-Kilo turning base for one-seven!"

"Roger, Two-Juliet-Kilo, no other reported traffic!"

I double-clicked an acknowledgment on the mike and asked Tim, "Electric fuel pumps on?"

"Check, pressure's green."

"Flaps ten degrees?"

"Check, flaps ten degrees!"

After flying for three days from Fairbanks, Alaska, to Shawnee, Oklahoma, my younger brother, Tim, was glad to get home. He's tired of me talking about my new three-axis strategy game that I call Chessnik.

"Gear down!"

"Gear coming down!"

"Shawnee Unicom, Aztec one-zero-two-Juliet-Kilo on final for one-seven!"

"Airspeed seventy-two knots. Do we have three in the green?"

"Negative, three in the green!"

"Say again!"

"Negative, we only have two in the green!"

Airspeed was okay, and I was right on glide, so I looked at the lights. And they indicated that the right main gear was not down and locked. I looked out the left window at the little mirror on the left engine nacelle and saw that the nose gear was truly down and locked! But I have no way to get a visual on the main gear. I wondered if another mirror somewhere would help. A major problem with low-wing aircraft is that you have no idea what is happening on the underside of the wings. Conversely, with high-wing aircraft, you have no idea what is happening on top of the wings. You can't win.

The numbers one-seven were coming up fast. I shoved the throttles and the mixtures to the wall, adjusted the trim, and dumped the flaps as my airspeed increased. I told Unicom I had to make a go-around and began to climb from about fifty feet off the ground. As we climbed, I cycled the gear up and then back down. The left gear light came on, then the nosewheel light came on. I turned on right downwind and trimmed out the plane; still there was no green light for the right main gear. I cycled the gear again and stretched out the downwind.

This is not happening, right? This happens to John Wayne and other people in movies, but not me.

Unicom called, "Two-Juliet-Kilo, is there a problem?"

Two green lights came on, and they leered like an evil grin. I rocked the wings back and forth. "Unicom, I'm going to leave traffic to the north. I can't get an indication that my right main gear is down."

"Roger, Two-Juliet-Kilo. Let us know if we can help."

"Thanks, Unicom!"

"Okay, Tim, what have you done wrong? It's the wheel on your side that won't come down."

"What? Me? All I did is pull the gear handle down."

"Maybe the light bulb is burned out. Switch it with one of the others."

Tim unscrewed the green bulb for the right main gear, dropped it, and fumbled around on the cabin floor, looking for it. He found it and switched it with the nose gear bulb. I cycled the gear again, but no green light for the right main gear.

"Well, it's not the light bulb. Let's see if Unicom will help. Unicom, this is Aztec Two-Juliet-Kilo."

"Two-Juliet-Kilo, this is Unicom, go ahead."

"Unicom, is there someone who can stand by the runway and take a look at our right main gear as we fly over and see if it looks like it's down and locked?"

There was a long pause, and I turned on a long final for one-seven.

"Aztec Two-Juliet-Kilo?"

"Roger, Unicom."

"We have a mechanic driving out there. He can tell if it's down, but not if it's locked."

"Roger, Unicom, I understand. That will help." I set up for a slow flight down one-seven.

"Uh, Jan, what are you going to do if the gear is not down?"

"Well, Tim, this plane is like a DC-3. It's made for gear-up landings. The main wheels hang down four inches when the gear is up. I'll feather the props to a horizontal position and glide to a landing on those four inches, and maybe there won't be too much damage to the nose. Are you going to throw up?"

"No! I'm too scared to throw up."

I mush down the runway ten feet up and just above a stall. We flashed by some people; their faces were just a blur. And I added full power.

As I turned on downwind, Unicom called, "Aztec Two-Juliet-Kilo?"

"Roger, Unicom."

"He says it's down in the correct position but has no clue if it's locked or not."

"Roger, Unicom, that helps. I think it's just the indicator switch. We're going to touch down this time."

"Roger, Aztec Two-Juliet-Kilo. I have the fire station on hold."

"Thanks, Unicom. We're on final for one-seven."

I approached at the bottom of the numbers, planning to keep the right gear off the ground until that wing quit flying. I saw people lined up outside the flight service station. People always come out to see you crash and burn. Tim was quiet.

The left main hit the ground, and then the nosewheel touched down. I had the pilot's wheel turned to the left, and I was giving it a hard right rudder. The Aztec slowed and settled on the right main with a slight groan, and we broke to a stop. The gear held. She was down and locked.

As we taxied in, the disappointed crowd dispersed. Tim was so hyped up, he wouldn't sleep for a week. He quipped, "Nice landing, Jan."

"Well, you know what they say. Any landing you can walk away from—"

"Yeah, I know, is a good landing. Mom will be pleased you didn't kill her baby on this trip." With that comment, he opened the door, hung his head out, and made retching sounds into the right engine's prop wash.

After tying the Aztec down and closing my flight plan, I crawled under the right wing and took a peek inside the wheel well. Bolted to the frame at the end of the wheel well was a small push-button switch. When the gear is down and locked, a small block of aluminum attached to the wheel strut closes that switch, and I get a green light in the cabin. On this last leg of a four-thousand-mile flight, that little block of aluminum had loosened and slid down the strut to a position where it barely missed the switch when the gear came down. How such a little thing could induce such anxiety was perplexing.

Down Under and Hot

Watching the sunrise over the South Pacific from thirty-five thousand feet, I reflected on how nice it would be to visit a warm, sunny beach while Fairbanks remained frozen in the last part of an arctic winter. An oil company out of Chicago had hired me to evaluate some drilling prospects in central Queensland, Australia. The field work was the best part, and a break from dealing with grizzly bears was greatly welcomed.

I began my trip attending a short conference on Australian geology in Surfers Paradise. I had read all the publications I could borrow or buy, and I was here to find out what might be new about the geology of Queensland. The area was beautiful, and I thought that the topless beach would really give the place some extra charm. The problem with a topless beach is the fact that everyone is topless, including grandma, great-grandma, the extremely plump, and those challenged by physique. People-watching was not as entertaining as I had thought it would be.

After four days in paradise, I caught a ride northward to Maryborough Downs. I spent the night as a guest in an old farmhouse that let me enjoy the full force of a tropical night in a rain forest. The screams, screeches, grunts, and terrifying cries didn't abate until dawn. I was uncomfortably tired as I got in a Land Cruiser and started driving on the wrong side of the road to Winton. About an hour later, the Land Cruiser overheated, and I pulled over at a roadhouse. A roadhouse in Australia is similar to a roadhouse in Alaska, being for the most part a convenience store with a bar. The fan belt was okay, and the water pump was not leaking.

Since the Land Cruiser had nearly 150 kilometers on it, I thought it was a good bet that the thermostat had gone bad. Lucky for me, there's a toolbox in the Land Cruiser. I removed the thermostat, and twenty minutes later, I was back on the road. And the engine was running much cooler.

As I drove westward, the trees got shorter until they were bushes, and open spaces were covered in grass. This was disappointing; the farther I go west, the more Australia looked like western Oklahoma. I reached Winton by sundown and got a room at the Matilda Hotel. Winton is one of the early opal-mining districts and the home of the "Waltzing Matilda" song.

I get an early start the next morning because I have some geologic stops to make. Right off, the road was busy with road trains and kangaroos. The road trains were big trucks with two or more trailers full of cattle, heading east toward the coast. I discovered that although there were posted speed limits, no one absolutely paid any attention to them. The kangaroos had their own agendas and had yet to learn of the dangers of road trains. The road trains almost blew me off the road, and if it was dusty, I had to pull off the road to let the dust from each one settle.

I made my first stop at Pat Malone's cattle station, and he was happy that it was getting cooler. It's expected to be only 102°F today; winter is coming on. One of his sons and one wee grandson told me that they killed three snakes this morning, and there were plenty about. I've done lots of fieldwork in heavy snake areas such as the American Southwest. I listened to them, but I was not overly concerned.

Three hours later, as I was slowly grinding my way over the grass in the outback at St. Elmo Downs, a big snake popped up its head and struck the right front tire on the Land Cruiser. It made a dull thump like someone had hit the tire with a small rock.

Whoa! Did I really see this?

It was hot, and I had the windows open because there was no air-conditioning in the Land Cruiser. I was wondering if a snake would try to come in a window. Slowly I continued my travel; a snake lifted its head two feet in the air above the grass and swayed from side to side. These snakes looked more like worms since they didn't have the triangular head of American or Mexican snakes.

I pulled into a rock quarry and stopped. I opened the door and leaned out and looked under the Cruiser. I checked my chosen path to the outcrop, and I didn't see any snakes. I got out and headed to a quarry wall. I was wearing high-top engineer boots and shorts that were cutoff jeans. *My white Alaskan legs should blind a snake*, I thought. All I had was my rock hammer; what I really needed was a machete. I had no gun, no machete, and bare legs; I felt naked.

I knocked a few pieces of rock off the back face of the quarry, and two snakes slid out from some loose rock and headed off into the grass. I stepped back and studied the rock samples, trying to place where I was in the stratigraphic section. Satisfied that I knew where I was in geologic time, I tossed the samples into the grass, and something slithered away. Well, at least, I didn't have to worry about bears. I stopped at another quarry and then headed on to Julia Creek for the night.

The next few days were hot, and I had, without a doubt, the worst sunburn on my legs I've ever had. In the evenings, I didn't bother to eat; I just headed to the hotel and lay in front of the air-conditioning unit. Living in Alaska had made me soft. Working in the Sonoran Desert of Northern Mexico some fifteen years ago, I would work all day in the heat like this and then party for half of the night.

The Sonoran Desert was hot and had lots of rattlesnakes, but the vegetation was the worst part. Everything had stickers (or thorns) on it. Some needlelike stickers had hooks or barbs that were painful to extract from your flesh. In Australia, if you see something like a cactus, you are required to kill and burn it.

I had found that various areas were easily accessible, and the fieldwork was going quickly. So today, I decided to check out a low priority anomaly that was thirty kilometers south of Julia Creek.

It was just after thirteen hundred hours when I checked in with the rancher who grazed his cattle on the area where I was headed. It was already 115°F, and I readily accepted an offered glass of iced tea. The hospitality offered by the Australians in the outback is marvelous. I was getting addicted to the little bars of lemon cake that often came with tea. The rancher took a big swig of his iced tea and said, "I gotta tell ya, mate, the dingos are gonna be the death of me." He ranted for a while then added, "Go anywhere ya want, son. Just be sure ya close the gates behind ya."

I assured him that I would close the gates behind me, just as I had at farms and ranches in other parts of the world.

Two more kilometers down the road, I turned westward on nothing but a dirt road that took me to my first gate in the dingo fence that protected his young calves. I was thankful that the rainy season was over. I could tell by the deep dried-out ruts that this road was a challenge when wet.

Wow, the dingo fence was three meters high (nearly ten feet) and made of woven hog wire. The gate was huge (went well with the fence), but the latch was just a chain looped through a hole in the hog wire. I reached through the hole and unhooked the chain from a hook. Something that felt like a hypodermic needle stung my left leg just above my boot top. I looked down at my leg and noticed a small snake, which dropped out of the fence. It hit the hot dirt and slithered off at high speed.

A snake in a fence was not a surprise because in Oklahoma and Texas, during the hottest part of the summer, snakes climbed up in fences, trees, and barn rafters. However, having a rattlesnake drop out of a tree right in front of you is a surprise you never get used to.

I started pushing the gate open and stopped about halfway. Wow, I felt dizzy, and my head hurt. I was standing there in the hot sun, feeling sicker by the second. I decided to return to the Land Cruiser, and as I locked the gate, I convulsed and expelled everything in my stomach. On the way back to the Land Cruiser, I convulsed so hard that I almost fell down. I did not recall having the dry heaves before. If this was that, it hurt my whole body.

As I pulled myself into the Land Cruiser, I noticed two small streams of blood steadily flowing out of my left leg just above my boot top. Sitting on the seat of the Land Cruiser, I dabbed at the blood with my handkerchief, and one small hole actually fountained blood. I closed the door and started driving on the dirt road. Halfway to the main road, I started convulsing again. I was shaking so hard that I stopped the Land Cruiser and started to slide out onto my feet. I doubled up in pain and fell on the ground. I was screaming and rolling on the ground because every nerve in my body hurt. Even my eyes hurt. Holding on to the door, I struggled to stand up.

I was covered in blood and dirt. I felt like I was suffocating while I felt around the seat, looking for my bottle of water. I couldn't find it; this must be what it felt like to die. I finally got myself pulled up into the Land Cruiser and drove to the main road. I didn't even look for road trains; I just drove on to the road and headed north to Julia Creek.

I made about a kilometer along the road when I noticed that it seemed to be getting dark. I stopped on the road and forced myself to take deep breaths. I had a headache that made me scream. All around the periphery of my vision, there was a dark cloud. I started slowly moving again, but all I could see was a small round area straight ahead. It was like looking through a tunnel. I felt very dizzy, so I stopped and took deep breaths. I closed my eyes and told myself that I was feeling better. I wanted to take a nap, but my skin felt so hot that I had thoughts about the stories of spontaneous combustion. I was sure that I was getting severely dehydrated, so I started driving again. I sped up until I could feel a little breeze, and that helped. I knew that there was a nurses' station in Julia Creek, but the question was *where*.

I drove into Julia Creek on the east end of town and spied the nurses' station on the right side of the street. I stumbled into a building that looked like it was right out of World War II, just a wood-and-fiberboard shack. I headed straight to a drinking fountain and started downing the precious fluid.

A thirty something woman with blond hair came out a door and inquired, "What happened to you, mate?"

"I think I've been snake bit," I replied.

She dragged me away from the delicious water and into the room she had just come from and sat me on a stool. She pulled off my boot and sock and asked, "Did we roll around in the dirt a bit?"

"A few times," I replied.

As she washed my leg, she asked, "What kind of snake?"

I told her, "I'm not sure, but it looked like a big worm about thirty centimeters long."

She looked up at me and said, "Sounds like a taipan. You're lucky to be alive."

That shocked me, so I added, "It was a small one."

She responded with "The juveniles are usually the worst. We say if you live through the first thirty seconds, you'll probably make it."

She sent me to the hotel with one clean leg with a small bandage on it. The next thing I remember was waking up feeling much better and extremely hungry.

On the edge of town north of the nurses' station was a KOA campground managed by a local man named Drum. He was a stocky individual who had lived all his life in Julia Creek, and his claim to fame was that he had never worn shoes in his life. One look at his large, lumpy, scarred feet and you could believe it.

Just before noon, I dropped by his place for some information. Over the past three weeks, he had been a bottomless source of information about the local people and places.

I told him about my encounter with the taipan, and he held up his right hand. The middle finger was missing. With a big toothless grin, he said, "Snake, when I was eighteen."

I felt sick thinking that I might lose my foot or maybe my whole leg. He must have guessed what was going through my mind because he added, "Infection. But not to worry, mate, I'm sure that the nurse made ya right."

I asked him about access to a creek a little more than two kilometers north of town. He took a swig from a can of ale and replied, "It's easy to get to, has a rock bottom, but has a few deep holes."

I thanked him and headed north on the road to the Gulf of Carpentaria. When I reached the creek, I parked just off the road and started hiking downstream. Gently dipping rocks made small riffles and rapids in the stream. This was perfect. I broke off chips of rock and studied them as I walked along the edge of the water. The water was clear enough that I saw a fish darting about in the pools. At a little riffle, I squatted down and chipped off a piece of rock. I was definitely over the crest of the structure, and now the rocks were dipping toward the north. As I stood up, I saw a log floating in the next pool.

The log struck me as being a bit odd because there were no trees nearby, just bushes. As I was staring at the log, it moved forward a bit and snapped at a fish or something. I was shocked! I'd never seen so many teeth in one place. It blinked an eye, and I took off, running back to the Land Cruiser. It was a saltwater crocodile; no one would believe this.

I drove straight back to Drum and told him what I saw. He gave me his toothless grin and laughed. "Oh yeah, mate. During the rainy season, they come up all the creeks."

The Gulf of Carpentaria is home to the largest saltwater crocodiles in the world. The record is thirty-three feet long. It had not occurred to me that they might come 150 kilometers upstream looking for cattle, humans, and kangaroos.

Four weeks later, a big ugly scab fell off my leg, leaving a hole about the size of a dime in my leg. I went to a longtime family physician back in Oklahoma. He looked at the hole and remarked, "Looks like a nicely healed snakebite. Where have you been this time?

Light Rain, Summer 2013

Warm sunny days in Alaska are so rare that when one comes along, you are lured into a euphoric state of mind, which seduces you into thinking it's going to last forever. It should last until the evening at least—but no, it doesn't happen that way.

Near midmorning on a beautiful sunny day, my grandson, David, and I flew to Fairbanks, Alaska, from the mine on Gold King Creek to get supplies and ferry people back to town. David did the flying on the first trip into town. We unloaded empty gasoline cans and filled the little Cessna 182 with supplies from the hangar. While he drove off to get gasoline and other supplies, I flew back to Gold King Creek with the first load of supplies.

As I taxied down taxiway Charlie for takeoff on runway two-right, the bright sun shining in my eyes made it difficult to see where I was going. I didn't think I even noticed any clouds to the south near Gold King Creek while I did my run up at the end of the runway and looked south for incoming traffic. The tower told me that I was cleared for takeoff.

I taxied onto two-right and gently shoved the throttle to the wall. The Cessna 182 easily accelerated while I pushed hard on the right pedal so the engine torque didn't take me off the left side of the runway. The airspeed reached seventy knots, and I gently pulled back on the yoke. This is one of the most thrilling moments in aviation, the point at which the wheels unstick from the ground and you make the transition from a speeding deer to a bird that's free to fly. Now the Cessna 182 rapidly gained airspeed, shedding the bonds of Earth and becoming a true vehicle of the air. At this point, I always had a smile in my heart because I was back where I belong—in the air.

I was headed north and only two hundred feet off the ground when the tower said, "Five-zero-three-seven-Delta, contact departure."

I contacted departure, telling them that I was off two-right and southbound as I raised the flaps a notch, pushing the yoke hard forward so I wouldn't stall.

Departure replied with "Three-seven-Delta, make a right turn and continue to climb on heading for one-one-zero."

"Roger, three-seven-Delta," I replied.

I turned on the heading, raised the flaps another notch, and let the Cessna 182 steadily climb into her element. This heading took me eastward over Fairbanks and toward the busy army base. I raised the flaps all the way up and slightly trimmed back the power and the engine rpms. A few more seconds and I was at 2,500 feet. At this point, departures told me to turn right on course.

"Roger, three-seven-Delta," I responded as I rolled through a nearly ninety-degree right turn.

I rolled out on a heading of 174 degrees, leveled the plane, and set the power and rpms to the cruise settings. Three-seven-Delta now becomes a beast with a purpose as her airspeed increases and her nose points toward her destination.

Before taxiing onto taxiway Charlie, I had listened to ATIS, getting recorded information on airport traffic and local weather. The only thing of note was the mention of light rain due south in front of the mountains. Smoothly flying at 140 knots, I saw only fluffy white clouds lazily floating along the front of the mountains. Farther away, off to the southwest, Mount McKinley was completely shrouded in clouds. Nothing seemed threatening as I crossed the lush green Tanana Flats.

The bright sunshine glinted off the multicolored oil slicks that covered the shallow lakes south of the Tanana River. A positive proof of the oil and gas seeps that dotted the Tanana Flats from Delta Junction westward to the village of Tanana.

At about one-third of the way across the flats, departure told me that radar service was terminated and to squawk VFR. I acknowledged the squawk change, and as I turned the knob to 1200, the wreckage of a B-24 bomber slid beneath me. Just off the right, I saw the Wood River Buttes; then immediately on the left, I passed the twisted fuselage of a Cessna 206. Such sights exemplify the fate of flying in Alaska.

The first turbulence bounced me in my seat as I crossed the Wood River. I radioed the gold mine, telling them that I was ten miles out and inbound for landing. The mine replied that there was heavy rain at the mouth of the canyon.

Heavy rain! What happened to the light rain!

The turbulence increased, and I throttled back to 120 knots. Individual rain showers were lined up along the mountain front. One large dark shower stuck out in the lineup; that must be where the mouth of the canyon was hidden.

I cut my airspeed to ninety knots and flew along the left, or east side, of the storm. From this location, I got a glimpse of the north end of the gravel airstrip that was four miles up creek from the mouth of the canyon. The bad news was that halfway up the airstrip, it was black with heavy rain. I thought I would just have enough time to slip in behind the first shower and land on the north end of the strip before the next heavy shower obscured it completely.

I lowered the flaps two notches and dropped my airspeed to eighty knots as I made a 360-degree turn. When I completed the turn, I flew into the mouth of the canyon behind the first shower. I caught sight of the end of the airstrip, lowered the flaps all the way, and changed the engine settings to maximum power. I trimmed the nose down and dropped the airspeed to seventy knots while battling severe turbulence and a twenty-degree crosswind. I aimed for the huge boulders at the end of the airstrip, which had been painted fluorescent orange.

Wham! The main gear hit the gravel safely beyond the boulders. As I bounced back into the air, I pulled the engine power and raised the flaps. Deprived now of all her power and most of her lift, three-seven-Delta smoothly rolled down the airstrip toward the mining camp. Then another wham as the right tire hit a sharp rock and blew out. Once again, I was fighting to keep three-seven-Delta going in a straight line. Soon we limped to a stop.

The rain was falling hard while strong wind gusts rocked the silent airplane. Another Alaskan bush flight had been completed in a not unusual manner for Alaska. Down the airstrip, I saw through the pouring rain that two young men in four-wheel-drive vehicles were headed toward us. Hard rain and strong winds couldn't stop them from retrieving the cargo and rescuing their grandfather from a 1958 Cessna 182.

This is the real Alaska.

Inertial Drive

When I was nineteen, I drew up plans for an inertial drive device that would move a vehicle without a prop, wheels, or rocket exhaust. I showed it to my physics professor at the university, and he said it wouldn't work. Several years later, I built a model, and it worked. It had a torque problem, which I solved. And many years later, I built a working model that had no inherent problems.

If you coupled this device to a long-lived supply of electricity (such as a thermonuclear reactor), you would have a propulsion unit that could drive you to the stars. When I tried to get a patent on the device, it was rejected by the patent office. I sent a video of the working model and three affidavits from professionals vowing that it really works to the patent office, and they still rejected it. I wonder if the Chinese would be interested.

A past student of mine from St. Gregory's University pointed out that a description of my inertial drive existed in the Bible. He was correct. It looked just like the wheel within a wheel device described in Ezekiel. One, this may mean that aliens visited Earth two thousand years ago, flying a ship powered with an inertial drive like mine, or two, someone had invented a time machine powered by my inertial drive and used it to visit places on Earth when they traveled back in time. Maybe it's me?

The Arctic Winter

I love:
    the beauty of the aurora borealis
    dancing across the black winter sky.
I love:
    the twinkle of fine ice crystals
    floating in the dead still air.
I love:
    the sharp intensity of minor odors
    made so by the freeze-dried air.
I love:
    the crystalline blanket of hoarfrost that covers all
    even me if I stand still too long.
I feel the solidity
    of the ice-covered rivers and lakes.
I sense the purity
    of the snow-covered landscape.
I delight to hear
    how sounds change
    with the increased density of the super cold air.
I love to make footprints
    in snow that is so cold
    it crunches like Styrofoam flakes.
I love to blow
    at the perpetual cloud of condensing breath
    that crystalizes on my parka's ruff.
Microscopic crystals that line

my fur-rimmed view of the winterscape
    with continuous twinkles of light.
I squint at the occasional rainbow-colored sundog
    that dots the twilight sky at noon.
I love to hear the silence,
    the indescribable quietness.
I hear the stillness of a remote frozen land
    where even time has been brought to a standstill.
You are engulfed with the silence,
    and as your ears adjust,
    you gradually become aware
    of a distant thudding noise.
This thudding gets louder
    until it reaches an annoying level.
It sounds as if it's coming from all directions!
You look around and inhale.
The passage of breath through your throat
    sounds like steam vented from a boiler.
You listen to the rhythm of the thudding,
    it sounds familiar
    it's the beating of your own heart.
Your heart sounds like
    it wants to burst from your chest.
Then you realize
    you hear it now because
    there are no external sounds
    to mask that engine of life
    beneath your breast.
It makes you further realize
    that as long as it thuds away
    you are alive.
If it stops, you're dead.
It makes you face the reality
    that you're mortal.
It makes you ever aware
    of the fragility of life.
It makes you understand
    that life is a special thing

because in the vastness
of this cold, frozen universe,
there are only a very few sparks of life.
That in turn makes you cognizant
that quality is the only thing
which gives meaning to life.

THE BUSH PILOT AT THE BAR

It was near midnight when
I entered a lodge's rustic bar.
In the Alaskan summer night,
    you'd not see a star.

The bar was filled with smoke
and several heavy drinkers.
One seemed unconscious—perhaps
    just one of those deep thinkers.

A tough-looking woman said,
"Hey, bozo, what'll you drink?"
A gin and tonic, oh no!
    Then just a beer, I think.

I found an empty wooden chair
near the outside door.
When I saw a three-legged dog
    lying on the floor.

"How did he lose his leg?"
I asked a drunk, expecting a lie.
"Ask the bush pilot at the bar,"
    was the surly sot's reply.

"How do I get to Yakutat?"
I asked a cigar-smoking redhead.
"Ask the bush pilot at the bar,"
between puffs, she said.

I tossed down my brew
and started back to the bar.
Someone gave me another beer
before I'd gone very far.

"How do I get to Yakutat?"
I asked he who gave me the beer.
"Ask the bush pilot at the bar,"
he bellowed in my left ear.

I tried to push toward the bar
when I felt a pull on my hat.
Facing a huge bald man, I asked,
"How do I get to Yakutat?"

He grinned, belched, and said,
"I sure do like yer hat.
But ask the bush pilot at the bar
about things like that."

I looked at that drunken rabble
at the crowded bar rail.
I couldn't tell who might be
a bush pilot without fail.

So I roared like a bear,
"Hey, who's the bush pilot here?"
A hush fell over the smoky bar;
they all turned to stare.

"Well now, I guess that's me,"
said a lady with blond hair.
The gender caught me off guard;
I gulped and gave her a glare.

Perhaps she was, so I asked,
"How do I get to Yakutat?"
"Brace yourself, honey." She winked.
"That's where you're at."

52109439R00068

Made in the USA
Middletown, DE
16 November 2017